PYTHON PROGRAMMING LANGUAGE FOR BEGINNERS

Learn Python from Scratch and Kickstart Your Programming Journey (2023 Crash Course)

Bert Daniels

CONTENTS

Introduction

Whether you're looking to improve your development abilities or start a new career as a software programmer, understanding Python is essential. There are several computer programming languages, as you are aware.

To conquer them all, you may require more than one life. So, why should you choose Python?

- It's long-lasting. This language isn't going away anytime soon, particularly with the growing need for Data Scientists.

- It's adaptable.

- That is applicable to everyone. Python code is compatible with all contemporary technologies.

- It is really simple to learn. In reality, an experienced programmer in any language can easily learn Python. It is really simple for novices to use and learn.

Python's syntax is simple; the language is high-level and has greater readability than most other languages. Also, it is simple to identify and repair Python problems, which is very important for novices.

You're off to a terrific start by reading this book. This book is intended to help you get started with Python programming. So, let's get started.

Chapter 1: History of Artificial Intelligence

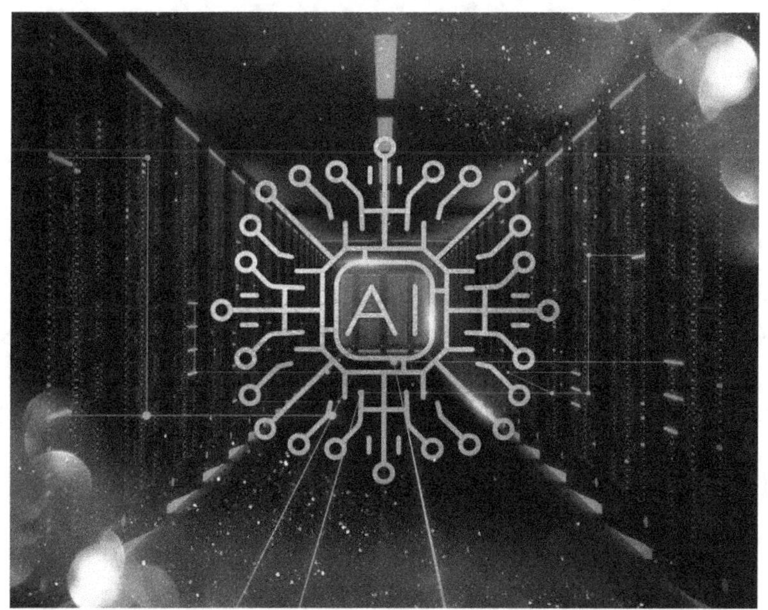

We begin by looking at early attempts to characterize artificial intelligence. For those unfamiliar with computer science and its allied subjects, the history of artificial intelligence may seem to be a dense and incomprehensible topic.

Regardless of how mysterious and impenetrable artificial intelligence seems, it is easier to comprehend than you may think when broken down.

So, what exactly is artificial intelligence, sometimes known as "AI"?

AI is a subfield of computer science that focuses on nonhuman intelligence or machine intelligence.

Artificial intelligence is based on the idea that human cognitive functions can be recreated.

During the 1700s and beyond, early thinkers advanced the notion of artificial intelligence. It grew more palpable throughout this time period.

Philosophers considered how intelligent robots may artificially computerize and modify the concept of human thought. The human thinking that sparked interest in AI culminated in the 1940s with the creation of the programmable digital computer. This specific finding pushed scientists to pursue the possibility of creating an "electronic brain," or artificially intelligent entity.

In addition, mathematician Alan Turing devised a test that determined a machine's ability to mimic human activities to the point that it was indifferent to human acts. Several theorists, logicians, and programmers expanded the present grasp of artificial intelligence as a whole beginning in the 1950s.

At this time, intelligence was thought to be the result of "logical" and "symbolic" thinking.

Computers used search algorithms to carry out the reasoning. At this period, the goal was to simulate human intellect by solving simple games and proving theorems. It soon became clear that these algorithms could not be employed to solve issues like robot movement in an unknown room. Extensive knowledge of the actual world would have been necessary to prevent a "combinatorial" expansion of the issue to answer.

In the 1980s, it was pragmatically agreed to limit the scope of AI to specific objectives, such as the reproduction of intelligent decision-making for the medical diagnosis of certain illnesses. This was the era of "expert systems," which could effectively reproduce a human specialist's intellect in narrowly specified areas.

Similarly, it became clear that certain intelligent operations, like text recognition, could not be accomplished using an algorithm constructed with a predefined sequence of instructions. Alternatively, it was conceivable to collect a large number of instances of the things to be recognized and then use algorithms to master the basic properties of these items.

That was the birth of what we now call "machine learning."

The computer learning phases might be characterized using probabilistic and statistical models as a mathematical optimization problem. Several of the learning algorithms used to simulate the human brain were dubbed "artificial neural networks."

Over the first four decades, AI has experienced moments of euphoria, followed by periods of unmet expectations. The early 2000s saw the first historical successes as a consequence of increased attention to particular issues and increased expenditure. AI systems have outperformed humans in some activities.

What is an Intelligent Machine?

With the invention of computers, the dispute over the nature of intelligence, which had occupied philosophers for thousands of years, assumed the shape of the title of this section. Alan Turing had addressed this issue several years before the Dartmouth workshop, and while looking for an answer, he proposed a "test," known as the "Turing Test," to determine machine intelligence.

Assume a person and a computer that purports to be intelligent are placed in the same room. Another person, a "judge," may communicate with them in written and verbal form, but they cannot see them. The judge interrogates the two interlocutors and determines who is and is not human. The judge's error demonstrates the machine's intelligence. It demonstrates that the machine is inextricably linked to an intelligent person.

This definition of intelligence eliminates many of the difficulties that might arise when attempting to define what intelligence is. We don't claim that the computer behaves like ourselves, just as we don't request that aircraft fly like birds. We are convinced that the machine cannot be distinguished from a person for a set of tasks that need what we term intelligence. The difficulty and breadth of the tests necessary to differentiate "Narrow AI" from "General AI" of future systems that should demonstrate human-level or greater intelligence for a wide range of activities.

The Current Nature of Artificial Intelligence

First, you must recognize that "true" AI does not exist now. A true AI system is one that can do all human-level tasks with equal competence.

Thus far, existing AI systems have been referred regarded as "narrow" AI. This implies that they can only provide relevant findings within a limited scope. Despite this, crucial components have been accumulating in recent years to propel AI beyond early adopters and into a broader market. Today's newspapers and publications are brimming with stories about the latest advancements in AI and machine learning technology. According to two assessments, artificial intelligence (AI) will become the biggest economic potential for enterprises and governments over the next several decades. AI advancements have the potential to improve global G.D.P. by 14% between now and 2030. This equates to an extra $14-15% trillion in productive contributions to development.

AI, like the steam engine, electricity, and the internet, may become a transformational technology over time. The market for AI acquisition will follow a broad S-curve structure, with a gradual start in the early stage. Although it is still in its early phases, AI is already providing tremendous benefits to those who have adopted the technology. Just 1% believe they have seen no significant value, while 78% believe they have seen a great benefit. The largest value was seen in risk management and manufacturing across all business processes.

Some of the Recent Progress in AI Text Generation

When it comes to text creation, the OpenAI GPT-2 Model can generate realistic text. Although there is a lot of excitement and ethical debate around this paradigm, below is a list of commercial applications related to text generation:

Fan Fiction Generation: Give a mode some background and let it construct an entire fiction around it, or apply ideas and continually direct it to produce a tale you like in no time.

Automatic News Generation: The news is often generated in response to an event on social media. For example, if Elon Musk sends a tweet, it is likely that it will become news and that multiple articles will be published about it. You can use real-time social media data to generate automated news.

Content Generation: This model may be used to gather a large quantity of stuff from the internet and display it on your blog. A single item is often distributed over numerous sites, allowing the model to rewrite the blog for you.

Customized Articles: You read news articles every day, but what if the content is tailored to your reading preferences? This has a major issue.

Automatic Storylines for Games: This may look futuristic, but it is conceivable if the model is trained on a large dataset of a world. The MCU model, for example, may release bespoke stories, which may be used for a different game ending for everyone who plays it!

Image Generation: Pictures represent a significant component of the internet. Many individuals, from graphic designers to concept artists, rely on visuals to communicate and earn a living.

Face Generation: Since it may be used to create realistic faces of nonexistent persons, this application may already be influencing the gaming industry. You may still use it to swiftly build the faces of children and complete family trees based on the game store line.

Anime Face Generation: Anime is a massive business in Japan, yet designing a character's face takes a long time. GANs (Generated Adversarial Networks) may be used to create a vast number of them with the press of a button.

Photography: Repairing shattered images, superzoom, noise reduction, and realistic nighttime shots are just a few of the advancements that are currently available in contemporary smartphones. This AI enables you to quickly become an expert in picture editing.

Audio Generation

Another kind of material that we utilize on a regular basis is audio. Whether you're conversing or listening to music from your favorite playlist. Here's a rundown of recent developments:

- **Composition and Synthesis of Music**: If you have a music sheet, you can make music with a variety of instruments, but what if AI could assist you in playing those musical instruments? You may go even further by allowing AI to write music as long as certain limits are met.

- **Synthesis of Speech**: Realistic voice synthesis has been a challenge, but with recent advances, you can now synthesize realistic speech. There is also a study on shifting one person's voice to another or even modifying what one person said.

Animation Generation

On today's internet, video is the most popular sort of material. YouTube is a popular site, and many YouTubers make money online by creating high-quality material.

- **Video Style Transfer**: You may convert one form of video to another, or if you're an artist or animator, you can write basic comments and let AI suggest some ideas.

- **Realistic Animation:** AI is also capable of animating things in a realistic manner. This may be utilized directly in the field of 3D animation to animate complicated objects without breaking a sweat. It also applies to in-game animations.

- **3D Modeling**: GANs may be used to construct a wide range of 3D models, including a huge number of synthetic characters and buildings.

There's little doubt that artificial intelligence will play a large part in day-to-day living as the future unfolds, from self-driving vehicles to healthcare diagnosis, stock market research, and minor tasks like file editing.

It may be a gradual shift as AI's capabilities expand to meet the problems that humans bring, but the shift is coming. Once that shift occurs, it will very certainly usher in a whole new age of technology and human progress.

Realistic Animation

Machine Learning (ML) has become a buzzword in recent years. Machine Learning has a wide variety of applications, from automating monotonous chores to providing insightful insights, and companies across the board try to benefit from it. You may already be using a machine learning-powered gadget. For example, a Fitbit-style wearable fitness tracker or an intelligent house assistant. Nevertheless, there are several more applications of ML.

Overview of the history of ML

ML is an essential component of contemporary business and research. It includes methods and neural network models to assist computer systems in gradually altering their performance. ML algorithms create a mathematical model utilizing sample data to make training choices without being instructed to do so.

Arthur Samuel, an IBM employee, created chess software in 1952. The algorithm could keep track of where it is and build an unspoken model that suggests better moves when they are needed. Samuel played around with the software and discovered it could improve over time.

With the software, Samuel defined the general providence characterizing computers' inability to transcend beyond written instructions and understand patterns in the same manner that humans do. As a result, he developed the phrase "machine learning," which he defined as: A branch of research that provides a computer with the capacity to learn without being overtly commanded.

Chapter 2: Introduction to Python Programming

The Python programming language is a sophisticated open-source language established by Van Rossum in the 1980s. The Python Software Foundation now maintains the language. Python is a powerful programming language that can be used to create games, online applications, and graphical user interfaces.

This is an advanced language. Reading and writing Python code is analogous to reading and writing standard English statements.

Python programs can't be run by machines right away because they aren't written in a way that machines can understand.

Python is an interpreted language. Python is an object-oriented programming language that lets users manage data structures to make and run applications. Almost everything in the Python programming language is a class. In the Python programming language, all objects, functions, classes, data types, and methods have the same location.

Programming languages are created to meet the needs of programmers and consumers who want an efficient way to construct programs that influence people's lives, economies, lifestyles, and society. They improve people's lives by increasing productivity, improving communication, and increasing efficiency. When languages fail to satisfy expectations, they die and become extinct, and more powerful languages replace them. Python is a programming language that has stood the test of time and remains popular across sectors, corporations, and programmers. It is a flourishing and important language that is suggested as a first programming language for individuals who wish to get started with programming.

The Ups of Using Python Language

The following are some of the reasons why you should learn and utilize Python over other languages:

Readability

Python programs utilize straightforward, clear, and concise instructions that are easy to follow, even for persons with little programming experience. As a result, Python applications are easier to debug, improve, and maintain.

The Least Learning Time

Python is simple to learn. Most people think that Python is a good first programming language because its codes are short and its syntax is easy to understand.

Expands Different Platforms

Python works on Mac OS X, Windows, and other operating systems, such as those on mobile devices. It also works with microcontrollers found in toys, remote controls, appliances, and other similar devices.

Installing Python

How to Install Python on Windows

To install Python on a Windows laptop, first, get the installation package of your choice from the Python main website.

You will be asked to download the most recent version of Python from the Python main website.

Also, if you're looking for a certain release, you may scroll down the page to find download links for previous versions.

Nevertheless, it is preferable to get the most recent version, which is Python 3.7.4, at the time of writing. But, your selection should always be based on what would be most useful for your project.

How to Install Python on Mac

If you have a Mac, you can still get the Python installation package from the Python main website.

How to Run the Installation File

When you've finished downloading, go to installation by double-clicking the downloaded.exe file. IDLE, documentation, and pip will be included in the standard installation.

Working with Python

Python is a dynamic and adaptable programming language that may be used in a variety of ways. You may use it interactively to test code or a statement on a line-by-line basis or to search its features. It can be used in script mode or to read an entire file of statements or an application program.

Interaction with the Command Line

Python is most often used via the command line. Python is simple to understand since it reacts to every command typed on the >>> prompt. That may not be the preferred method of interacting with Python, but it is the quickest way to learn how it works.

Starting Python

Depending on the sort of operating system on your computer, there are many ways to access Python's command line.

- If you are using the Windows operating system, go to the start menu and choose the Python command line.
- You will use the Terminal Tool if you are working on Linux, Mac OS, or Unix.

Commands in computer programming languages tell the computer how to execute instructions. Thus, if you want to accomplish anything in Python, you'll need to put down a number of instructions. Python then converts the instructions such that they may be performed by the machine.

How to exit Python

You may leave Python by entering the following commands:

quit ()

exit ()

Control-Z, then enter

Integrated Development Environment (IDLE)

This utility is included in the Python installation package. You may, however, search for complicated third-party IDLEs if you like.

The IDLE provides a great framework for writing code and working with Python. The IDLE may be located in the same directory as the command line icon. To open the Python Shell window, click the IDLE button.

The Python Shell Window

This window has many dropdown menus as well as a >>> prompt. You may begin entering statements for execution after you sign in to the Python Shell window. But, the editing menu in IDLE enables you to return to prior commands. The Python Shell Window's menu includes options such as Edit, File, and Help.

The Shell and Debug menus each offer unique functionalities that are useful for developing complicated applications.

You may retrieve the most recent reset or even restart the shell from the Shell menu.

The Debug Menu has the right menu options for looking at the source file of an exception and choosing the error line. The debugger option will display an interactive debugger window that will aid in the execution of the code. The stack viewer option displays a new window that describes the current Python stack.

The Option will assist you in configuring the IDLE to your specific Python working preferences. The Help menu item includes documentation and a Python Help window.

The File Window

The choices on the File menu allow you to create a new file, a module, or an existing file and save your session. When you choose the 'New File' option, you will be sent to a new window with a basic and standard text editor in which you may write or change your code.

This filing window is initially named 'untitled,' but once you save your code, its name changes.

The menu bar in the File window varies differently from that in the Shell Window. It removes the 'Shell' and 'Debug' menus from the Shell Window, but it adds two new lists: the Run and Format menus.

When you execute your code in the file window, the Shell Window shows the output.

The Script Mode

While working in script mode, you do not see the outcomes as quickly as you would in an interactive manner. To observe the result of a

script, execute it and then use the print ()
function from inside your code.

Python Syntax

Python syntax is concerned with how human
users and the system should write and
understand a Python program. If you want to
create and execute your program in Python, you
must first learn the syntax.

Keywords

Keywords in Python are reserved words that
must be utilized in your code as variables,
function names, constants, or identifiers. If you
don't want to encounter mistakes while
implementing your application, keep the
following keywords in mind:

Break, def, lambda, is, not, tray, with, yield, exec, del, else, and, finally, print, while, return, try, pass, global, import, assert, class

Python Identifiers

A Python identifier is a name that is given to a function, variable, module, or another object in your Python program.

Since it will be a part of your program, each object you utilize in Python should be properly labeled or recognized.

The following Python naming conventions are essential to understand:

- An identifier may consist of a combination of capital characters, underscores, lowercase letters, and numerals between 0 and 9. (0-9). As a result, the following identifiers are correct: my variable, myClass, var 3, and print hello world.

- Distinctive characters such as @,%, and $ are not permitted in identifiers.

- A number should not be the first character of an identifier. As a consequence, whereas variable 2 is incorrect, variable 2 is fine.

- Python is a case-sensitive language, which should be extended to identifiers.

- Python keywords cannot be used as identifiers.

- To separate numerous words in your identifier, use underscores.

- The class identifiers begin with an uppercase letter, while the whole identifiers begin with a lowercase letter.

Even after a lengthy delay, you should always use identifiers that are practical. As a result, although it is simple to set your variable to c = 2, you may find it more helpful for future reference if you use a longer and more fitting variable name, such as num = 2.

Use Quotations

Python allows you to display string literals using quotation marks. You may use triple quotes, double quotes, or single quotes, but you must start and finish the string with the same kind. When your chain crosses many lines, you may use triple quotes.

Python Statements

Statements are instructions that may be executed by a Python interpreter. When you assign a value to a variable, such as my variable = "dog," you are generating an assignment statement. An assignment statement is as simple as c = 3. Other statement types in Python include while statements, if statements, and for statements.

Indentation

Braces are used to define blocks of code in most computer languages, such as Java. Python programs, on the other hand, are distinguished by their usage of indentation. Python code chunks are indented. As a consequence, Python code is simple to comprehend and read.

When indenting code blocks, ensure sure the indentation gap is consistent. If you enter your code in an IDE, Python provides a standard guideline that regulates the usage of indentation.

In general, the indentation should be about four spaces to the right.

Comments

While developing software, you will find that it is best practice to add some code explanations. Here is where your feedback comes into play. A comment is a way to make sure that your code is easy for other programmers to understand. Additionally, when you review your code after a few months, you will not be confused about what a certain line of code was accomplishing. The hash symbol is used to write comments in Python. When the Python interpreter runs the code, the hash symbol tells it to disregard the comment.

Chapter 3: Variables and Data Types

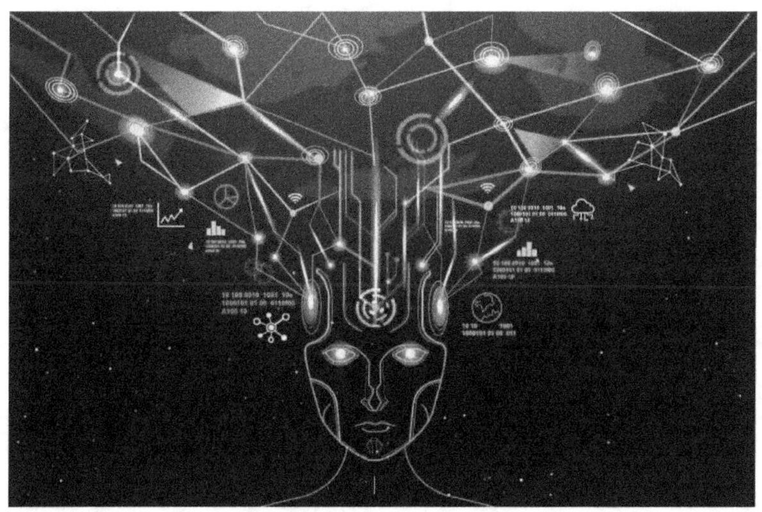

Python applications are stored using the.py file suffix. In other words, the file name for the hello program should be hello.world.py. This automatically displays the file's Python scripts. Your editor then runs the file via the Python interpreter, which scans through the program and determines the meaning of each word. For example, when the interpreter sees the word print, it shows whatever is inside the brackets on the screen.

Your editor highlights various areas of your program in different ways as you write it. For example, it recognizes "print" as the name of a function and displays that word in blue. It recognizes that "Hello, World." is not Python code and displays it in orange. This feature is called syntax highlighting, and it is essential when you start writing your programs.

Variables

A variable is similar to a container that contains values that may be accessed. It is a way to talk about a part of memory that a certain program uses. Variables are used to help the computer store and get information from memory.

When it comes to variables, Python varies from other programming languages. Variables are linked to a particular data type in languages such as Java, C++, or C. In other words, it can only hold a certain kind of data. As a result, when a variable is of type integer, you can only store integers within it while running the program.

When it comes to variables, Python is quite versatile. As a consequence, Python allows you to modify the value and data type while the program is running. Let us now execute a Hello World program using a variable. Then, add a new line at the beginning of the file and alter the second line. The program will look like this:

```
"Hello, world!" text

print (text)
```

If you execute the following code in your Python editor, you should get the following output: Hello, world!

The variable text has been used in this program to store the value, which is the information connected to that variable. The value in the following example is the string "Hello, world!"

The effort for the Python interpreter is increased by adding a variable. After processing the first line, it links the text "Hello, World!" with the variable text. As it reaches the second line, it displays the value associated with a message on the screen.

Let's extend the above software by adding a second message to it. Include the following code lines:

"Hello, World!" text

```
print(text)
```

```
text="Hello Python beginner!"
```

When you run the code above in your Python editor, you should see two lines of output:

```
print(text)
```

Hey there, World!

Hi, Python beginner!

However, you may change a variable's value in your program at any moment, and Python will always remember its current value.

How to Name and Use Variables

While using variables in Python, you must follow a few rules and standards. You will get an error if you violate the rules.

Additional instructions allow you to develop code that is easy to read and comprehend.

Among these rules are the following:

- Only underscores, characters, and digits are permitted in variable names. A variable name must begin with a letter or an underscore, not a number. For example, a variable message 1 may be called.

- There can't be any spaces in variable names, but you can use underscores to separate words. For instance, num year but num year would result in mistakes.

- Variable names should not include Python keywords or function names. In other words, do not utilize terms reserved by Python for a specific programmatic purpose, such as the phrase "print."

- Variable names should be brief yet descriptive. For example, the name is superior to n, while the num year is superior to the n year.

- Use caution while using the lowercase letter l and capital letter O since they are easily confused with the digits 1 and 0.

It may take some experience to grasp how to construct proper variable names, especially as you progress. You'll become better at designing meaningful names as you create more programs and look through other people's codes. Last but not least, computers are strong, but they do not distinguish between excellent and poor spelling. This implies you don't have to adhere to English and grammatical conventions when attempting to generate variable names.

The most common programming mistakes are single-character typos on a single line. If you spend a long time looking for one of these faults, know that you're not alone. Most experienced and brilliant programmers spend endless hours looking for problems of this kind.

Implementing new programming ideas in your own programs is the easiest way to learn them. If you get stuck while doing an activity, try something else for a time.

Strings

Python works with several data types to satisfy programmers' and application developers' demands for relevant data. They include Booleans, time, numbers, dates, and times. A string is a series of Unicode characters that may include letters, special symbols, and numbers.

You may define a Python string by enclosing it in single or double quotations.

```
>>> stringone = 'I am enclosed in single quotes."
>>> stringtwo = "I am enclosed in double quotes."
```

A string is a data type in Python.

A string is a "sequence of characters" that may be defined.

Characters are arranged in a certain order inside a String. For example:

Greeting = "Hello".

The first letter in the above string is 'h,' followed by 'e,' and so on.

The following string has the same characters; however, they are in different positions:

"loleh" means "hello."

How to Access the Individual Characters Inside a String

Some programming tasks will need the use of individual characters contained inside a string. A for loop may be used to separate distinct characters inside a string. Within your loop, the highlighted variable will take on each character in your string one at a time. For example, in "Maria," for c:

print (c)

>> M

>> a

>> r

>> i

>> a

Using individual characters in a string to do computations

It is simple to conceive how you can investigate the intricacies of a string now that you can iterate over it.

String Indexing

Another way to examine a string is to use indexing notation.

Indexing is a method of referring to particular items inside a string based on their location.

An index may be calculated by inserting an integer value between a pair of square brackets directly after the variable:

```
Word = "superman"
Print (word[0])
>> s
```

String indexes begin at zero.

Iterating a String Using Indexing

To iterate through the characters in a string, use a "for" loop. For example:

word = "hello" in word: print (c)

Nevertheless, if you want to traverse the string using indexing, you must build a range of integers that correspond to the indexes you want to visit. As an example:

print word = "hello" for I in range (0, 5): (word[i])

String Immutability

Immutable data types include strings. In other words, once generated, they cannot be changed. What really happens behind the scenes is that

Python creates a new string in computer memory and refers to it instead of the old one.

'Superman' as a name

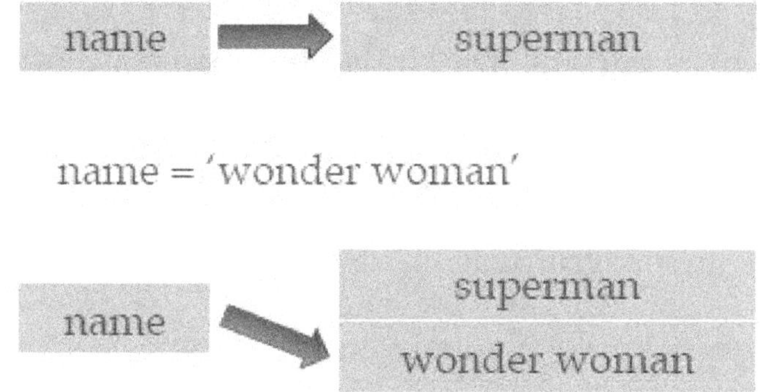

In other words, using notation to change single characters inside a string is impossible. You may cause an exception.

word = "Superman"

word[0] = "X" # exception!

Changing a String

To alter a string, you must first create a new String variable.

The changed version of the string may then be stored in this new variable.

Take, for example, the following programming challenge:

"Create a program that uses the underscore character to replace all vowels in a String."

You may first believe that you can just use String indexing to alter the characters in question. As an example:

word = "hello"

word(1) = "_"

word(4) = "_"

But since strings are immutable, this will not work!

To "create" the new String, you must first establish a new string variable to hold the modifications and then use a loop to examine every character in a sequence. As an example:

word = "hello"

newword = ""

for c in word:

if c == 'e' or c == 'o':

newword += "_"

else:

newword += c

String Functions

Thus far, you've learned about numerous functions that may be used with strings. The len () function, for example, may count the number of characters in a string.

Apart from that, there are additional functions that you may use while working with Strings to make things easier for you as a developer.

Identifying the Biggest and Smallest Characters in a String

The greatest and smallest characters in a string may be calculated using Python built-in methods. As an example:

```
a = max("python")
b = min("python")
print ("max:", a)
print ("min:", b)
>> y
>> h
```

String Slicing Notation

To trim a string in Python, you must use a bracket symbol to specify the index range of the characters you want.

The following syntax is represented by the standard notation:

```
substring = bigstring[start:end:step]
```

At least one index value must be included.

Substring characteristics include all of the characters from the start value to the end value.

When you remove a starting index value, Python assumes you want to start at the beginning of the string or continue slicing the last piece of the string. This should look similar to the function range.

String Operators

Now that you know how to use the "+" and "*" operators with a String.

The "+" operator may be used to join two strings together.

The "*" operator may be used to specify how many times a String should be repeated.

Testing String Using "in" and "not in"

The "in" operator is a Boolean operator used to detect if a substring occurs inside another string. For example, when you use the "in" operator to make an expression, the result is a Boolean.

```
word = "Jackson James John Chris Tom"if "Chris" in word:print ("found him!")
else:
print ("can't find Chris")
```

String Method

A "method" is a function that is a member of an "object" that performs operations on that object. As an example:

We haven't spoken much about objects in the class, but strings may be a fantastic way to get started with methods and objects.

The standard syntax is as follows:

stringvariable.method(arguments)

String Validation

String testing techniques allow you to check whether a certain pattern exists inside a given string variable. As an example:

```
word = '1234'if word.isdigit() == True:print ("All chars in word are digits!")else:print ("Not all ch
```

The "isdigit" technique is used to call "word" in this example. The following function returns True if all characters in a string are numeric digits, and False otherwise.

String Modification Methods

Bear in mind that strings are immutable and cannot be modified directly.

But they have many "modification" methods that change the string and return a new copy of the string with the change.

```
word = "Craig"
newword = word.lower()
print (word)
>> craig
```

Searching and Replacing

Applications must typically search and substitute operations on data, similar to the "find and replace" feature seen in word processors.

The find () and index () methods may be used to search for strings and substrings in strings.

If the substring cannot be discovered, the find function returns -1.

If the substring cannot be found, the index () gives an error.

Searching a Specific Section of a String

The find () and index () methods both search from the beginning of the string to discover the occurrence of the substring.

You may optionally provide a start and end index to verify just a section of the text.

How to Search Backwards Through a String

The rindex () and rfind() methods function similarly to find() and index(), except that the text is searched backward from the end.

Centering Text

s.center(w, [pad]) centers the text inside a w-width field.

The optional pad character will be appended to the string's ends.

Concatenation

Strings may be concatenated with the + operator.

>>> 'welcomehome' + "home' = 'welcomehome'

Join Method

Strings, like numbers, have a join () function.

Multiplications

Integers can even be multiplied by strings.

>>> 'ship' * 5

Methods of Extracting Information About a String

s.count(ss) counts the number of times the substring ss appears in a string. s.endswith(sfx) validates whether a string ends with the substring sfx.

Chapter 4: Conditional Execution

There are times in life when making a choice is unavoidable. When it comes to programming, this is no exception. That is the same for every software that must assess a relevant issue. It is impossible to program without using branches in the program flow.

In programming and scripting languages, conditional statements are used to do different calculations based on whether or not a given condition evaluates to true or false.

Arithmetic and comparison phrases are often used in the condition. The expressions are evaluated as either False or True. Conditional statements, which are also called "conditional constructions," are statements that depend on the choice.

The if-then syntax is sometimes known as the if-then-else syntax. This is ubiquitous in most computer languages; however, the syntax varies per language.

Every programming language has conditional statements.

Conditional statements let you write code that may or may not execute based on the program's input.

When you completely run each statement in a program, moving from top to bottom with every line processed, you are not asking the program to do specific actions. Conditional statements allow programs to determine if a certain condition is satisfied and then determine what to do next.

There are several situations in which conditional statements are useful:

- If a student scores more than 65% on her test, her grade is passed; otherwise, her grade is failed.

- Determine a 5% discount if customers buy 10 mangoes or more. If people buy less, they don't.

- Calculate the interest if he has money in his account; if he doesn't, impose a fee.

You are developing conditional code when you evaluate conditions and allocate code to execute regardless of whether those criteria are satisfied or not.

Python conditional statements will be covered in this chapter.

In most programming languages, the if statement is one of the most often used conditional statements. It assesses whether or not a particular statement should be performed. When the statement checks for a certain condition and finds that it is true, the code it contains is run.

The if condition computes a Boolean expression and runs the block of code only when it is TRUE.

The condition will be converted to a Boolean expression based on the syntax of the statement (true or false). If the condition is true, the statement within the if block is performed; if the condition is false, the program inside the if block is not run.

The if statement's flow chart is shown below:

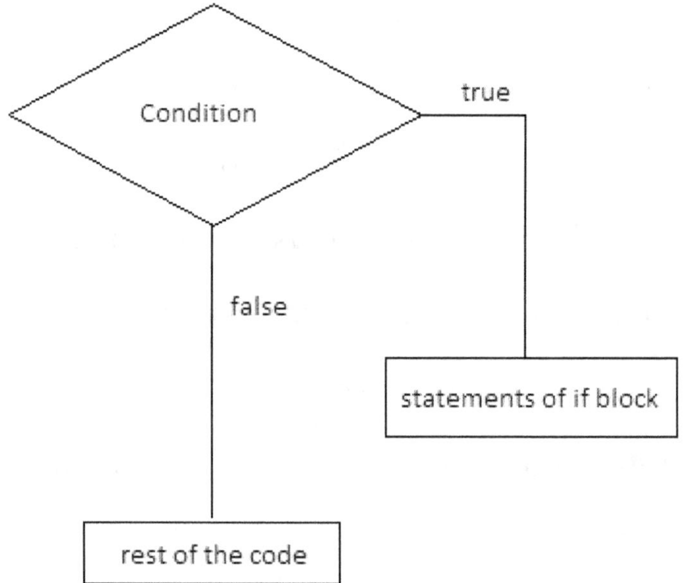

According to the flowchart above, the first controller will reach an if condition and assess if the condition is true; if the condition is false, the statements will be implemented; otherwise, the code inside the block will be performed.

If-else Statements

If a specified condition is discovered to be true, then the statements within the if block is executed; if the condition is false, then the statements inside the otherwise block are executed.

The otherwise block will be executed only if the condition becomes false; this is the block in which you will do certain actions if the condition is not true.

If the condition is True, the if-else statement computes the Boolean expression and performs the block of code available within the if block, and when the condition is false, it executes the block of code available inside the else block.

The syntax is as follows:

If (Boolean condition):

Code snippet

otherwise: the code block

The condition will be applied to a Boolean expression in this situation.

If the condition is determined to be true, the statements contained within the if block will be implemented; if the condition is found to be false, the statements included inside the program will be implemented.

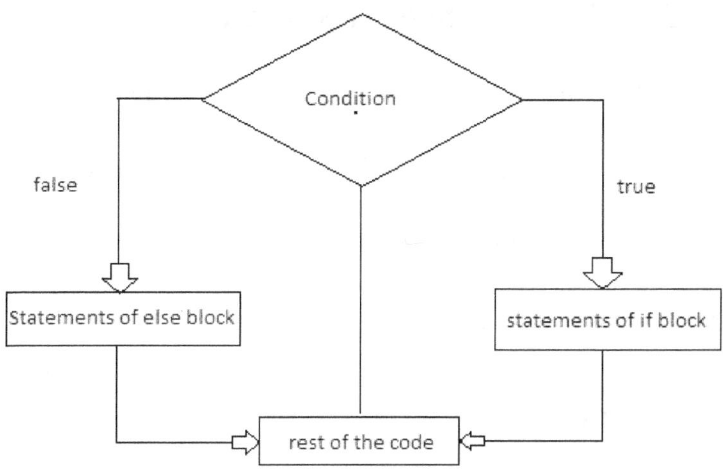

Let's have a look at the flowchart above.

If you pay close attention, you will notice that the first controller will reach the if condition and check whether the condition is true; if it is, the statements of the if block will be implemented; otherwise, the block will be executed, and the remaining code outside the if-else block will be implemented.

The Nested if –else Statements

Nested if-else statements are if statements or if-else statements that are accessible inside another if or if-else block. Python also has this characteristic, which will allow us to confirm numerous conditions in a single application.

An if statement exists inside another if statement that exists within another if statement, and so on.

Nested if Syntax

The following is the syntax:

If (condition): #statements to be executed if the condition is met

If (condition): #statements to run if the condition is met

#ending nested if #ending if

The grammar above clearly reveals that the if block will include another if block, and so on. The if block may include an 'n' number of if blocks.

Have a look at the following program:

If (number >0), number =10.

("This number is greater than ten")

If (number 10) is less than 10, print "This number is less than 10."

In the above example, a variable number with the value 10 is defined.

It will first validate that the first statement is true, then run the block of code included inside the first statement, then decide if the second if statement is true, and so on.

Elif ladder

You've heard of elif statements, but not the elif ladder. A ladder of elif statements is constructed in the manner of a ladder, as the name indicates.

when (condition):

#Statements that will be executed if the condition is true elif (condition):

#Statements that will be performed if the condition is false and if the condition is true elif (condition):

#Collection of statements to run when both the if and first elif conditions are false and the second elif condition is true elif (condition):

#Collection of statements to be performed if the first, second, and third elif conditions are false and the third elif statement is true, otherwise:

#Collection of statements to be performed when all if and elif conditions are false is useful when testing numerous expressions.

Example of elif ladder

my_marks = 89

if (my_marks < 35):

print ("Sorry!!!, You are failed in the exam")

elif(my_marks

< 60): print("Passed in Second class")

elif(my_marks

> 60 and my_marks < 85):

print ("Passed in First class")

else:

print ("Passed in First class with distinction")

The elif ladder is shown in this application. Initially, the control enters the if statement and assesses if the condition is true; if it is, the set of statements within the if block is implemented; otherwise, it is bypassed, and the controller proceeds to the first elif block and computes the condition.

The same procedure will be followed for the remaining elif statements, and if all of the if and elif conditions are determined to be false, the else block will be performed.

The if-else in a Single Line

With Python, you can still create if and elif expressions on a single line without worrying about indentation.

If Statement in a Single Line

We know how to construct if statements, as seen below:

If (condition): #list of sentences to execute if the condition is true

In Python, it is acceptable to write the preceding block of code on a single line.

As an example:

If statement 1; statement 2; statement 3;...statement n

If the condition is met, perform statement 1, statement 2, and so forth.

None of the statements will be performed if the condition is not met.

a single line of elif statements

syntax

if(condition): #list of statements to execute if the condition is met.

elif(condition1): #a set of statements that will be executed if the condition is met.

S else:

#list of sentences to execute if condition and condition1 are both false

This block may still be written in the manner described below:

if (condition): #Collection of statements to run if condition is true

elif (condition1): #Set of statements to run if condition1 is true; otherwise, #Set of statements to run if condition and condition1 are both false.

There may also be many statements; just separate them with a semicolon (;)

If (condition), then: statement 1; statement 2; statement 3;...;statement n else: statement 1; statement 2; statement 3;...;statement n elif (condition): statement 1; statement 2; statement 3;...;statement n

If statements with multiple conditions

It is not just feasible to express one condition inside an if statement; it is also possible to examine many conditions in an if statement, as seen below:

num 1=10 num 2=20 num 3=30 if (num 1== 10 and num 2== 20 and num 3== 30); print ("All conditions are met")

In this example, the if statement evaluates several conditions using the AND operator, implying that only when all criteria are true will the statements inside an if block be implemented.

It is also feasible to define the OR operators.

As an example:

namefruit is an abbreviation for "Apple."

if (namefruit == "Mango," "Apple," or "Grapes"):

In this example, just one of the three requirements is true, which is the rule of the OR operator. If any of the conditions is true, the condition is true, and the statement contained inside the if block is executed.

Let's look at a real-world example to figure out how many days there are in a month. You are aware that the number of days will vary in a leap year. This is shown programmatically using if, elif, and else statements.

```python
currentYear = int(input("Enter the year: "))
month = int(input("Enter the month: "))
if ((currentYear % 4) == 0 and (currentYear % 100) != 0 or (currentYear % 400) == 0):
        print ("Leap Year")
        if (month == 1 or month == 3 or month == 5 or month == 7 or month == 8 or month == 10 or month == 12):
                print ("There are 31 days in this month")
        elif (month == 4 or month == 6 or month == 9 or month == 11):
                print("There are 30 days in this month")
        elif (month == 2):
                print("There are 29 days in this month")
        else:
                print("Invalid month")
elif ((currentYear % 4) != 0 or (currentYear % 100) != 0 or (currentYear % 400) != 0):
print ("Non Leap Year")
        if (month == 1 or month == 3 or month == 5 or month == 7 or month == 8 or month == 10 or month == 12):
                print ("There are 31 days in this month")
        elif (month == 4 or month == 6 or month == 9 or month == 11):
                print("There are 30 days in this month")
        elif (month == 2):
                print("There are 28 days in this month")
        else:
                print("Invalid month")
else:
        print("Invalid Year")
```

Output:

```
Enter the year: 2020
Enter the month: 4
There are 30 days in this month
```

Output: 2

```
Enter the year: 2020
Enter the month: 1
There are 31 days in this month
```

Output: 3

```
Enter the year: 2019
Enter the month: 2
There are 28 days in this month
```

Output: 4

```
Enter the year: 2020
Enter the month: 2
There are 29 days in this month
```

Boolean Expressions

A Boolean expression may have one of two values: true or false.

False and True are the most basic Boolean expressions. A Boolean expression is one that compares numeric expressions for equality. The most basic type of Boolean expressions uses relational operators to compare two expressions.

A legal statement such as 5 10 is meaningless since it is always true. Readers are less likely to be perplexed by the term. Yet, since variables are dynamic, the value they retain throughout the execution of a program is destined to change.

Iteration

Iteration in programming refers to the repeating of lines of code. It is a necessary property in computer programming that aids in problem-solving. The main pillars of algorithm development are iteration and conditional execution.

Let us begin with the following:

Statement While

What if you wanted to develop software that could count up to 10,000? How are you going to address this problem? Will you take the time to write 10,000 printing statements? While you can, it will take a significant amount of time. Computers, on the other hand, often count; in fact, computers may count incredible quantities. Therefore there must be an escape route. You must print the value of a variable and then continue the operation until you reach 10,000. Looping is the process of repeatedly running the same code. Python includes two specific statements that manage iteration: while and for.

Here's an example of a program that makes use of the while statement.

num = 2 and num = 5:

num + print (num) = 1

The while statement in the above program will show the variable num on a regular basis. This code piece is then executed four times by the application.

count + print (num) = 1

The software increments the num variable by one after each output.

After four executions of the code, the condition becomes false, and the block of code is no longer implemented.

The line while num <= 5: begins the while statement. The condition that determines whether the block should be run comes after the while keyword. The program will continue to execute the block of code as long as the condition's conclusion is true. The loop, however, ends when the condition evaluates to false.

Also, if the condition is determined to be false at the start, the program terminates.

The while statement's conventional syntax is as follows: while condition: block

While is a Python-reserved word that starts the while statement.

The condition determines whether or not the body will be executed.

The condition will be followed by a colon (:).

The block is made up of one or more statements that must be performed if the condition is met. Any statements that complete the block must be indented one level further than the while statement's initial line. In general, the block belongs to the while statement.

Beginners may mix up the while statement and the if statement because they look the same. Occasionally, they may utilize if when they wish to use a while statement. As a result, novice programmers should be aware of the use of the while and if statements.

The running program implements the condition before executing the while block and then validates the condition after the while block for the while statement. If the condition stays true, the program will continue to run the code inside the while block until the condition is false. At this moment, the loop's execution ends.

Definite and indefinite loops

Let's explore the following code snippet:

```
n = 1

while n <= 10:

print(n)

n + = 1
```

Determine the number of iterations in the preceding software section. If you carefully examine this code, you will see that there are ten iterations. As a result, this loop is considered to be definite since you can precisely predict how many times it will run.

Have a look at the following code:

```
terminate = int (input ()))

print (n)

n += 1
```

The number of iterations for this code is impossible to determine. This number is determined by the user's input. But you can calculate how many times the while loop will repeat when the user provides input before the next execution starts...

While statements are often preferred for indefinite loops.

The for Statement

The while loop may be used to create indefinite loops. Originally, a while loop was used to perform a certain loop, such as:

```
n = 1
while n <10;
print(n)
n += 1
```

The print statement in the above code snippet will only be executed 10 times. To control the loop, three parts of code are required. It is the initialization, verification, and updating.

Python includes a useful technique for displaying a specific loop. The for statement loops over a set of values. A tuple may be used to show a series. As an example:

print for n in 1, 2, 3, 4, 5, 6, 7 (n)

The preceding code will behave just like the while loop in the previous section. The print command is executed 7 times in this example. The code will print the number one first, then the number two, and so on. The most recent value displayed is 7.

The for statement varies from the while statement in that it expects a collection of characteristics to be repeated. For example, you may want a loop that iterates across various integers, such as integer values ranging from 1 to 10. Although it is possible to construct a counter inside a while loop to guarantee this occurs, the statement is intended to handle this kind of situation quickly and effectively. Consider the hello world program. Using a for loop, this program will print the string five times. To do so, you'll need to understand the range function.

in range(5) for x:

("Hello, World!") print

The range allows you to access various numbers quickly.

When paired with a for a statement, it generates a loop that runs a certain number of times. The preceding software will print the string "Hello, World!" five times. It does this by assigning a specific value in the specified range to the new variable x for each loop iteration. If you recall how the following indices are generated using string character locations, you'll recall that they start at zero. Consider the following code as an example:

X in range for x (5)

("The value of x is 0.").

format(x))

When the for function is used with the range built-in function, each loop iteration changes x to the next value in the range requested.

It's as though you're manually requesting a counter using a while loop. The for loop automatically takes the next value, the variable x obtains a new value, and the inner code block is implemented.

Python Continue, Break and Pass

In Python, control statements are used to manage the order of execution of the program based on the logic and values.

Python offers three kinds of control statements.

-Continue

-Break

-Pass

In summary, this chapter has looked at conditional statements and iteration statements in Python. These are statements that impact the flow of a program's execution.

Conditional statements, such as if, if-else, elif, nested if, and many more, may affect the execution of a program.

If the statement computes a Boolean expression to true or false, the statement inside the if block will be implemented if the condition is true. But, if the condition is false, the statement included inside the else block will be performed only if you have typed it.

We also have an elif statement, which combines the else statement with an if statement and executes based on the prior if or elif statements.

Notes:

- Python has conditional statements that may be used for verification and validation.

- Python offers two forms of looping statements that aid in the repetition of a certain piece of code or statements.

- When you don't know how many times you need to iterate, you use the "while loop," and if you know how many times you need to repeat, the "for loop" is ideal.

- Python additionally has three control statements that enable you to direct the course of a program's execution.

Chapter 5: Python Functions

This chapter will walk you through Python functions. At the conclusion of this chapter, you will be able to write Python functions, call Python functions, and much more!

First and foremost, functions are an essential component of the Python programming language. You've already seen various Python functions, such as built-in features and jobs that come with their own libraries. But, as a Data Scientist, you will often need to build your own functions to tackle problems that arise when working with data.

That is why this chapter will take you through Python routines.

Let's get started:

Functions in Python

Python functions are required to control inputs and outputs in applications. All programming languages are designed to execute data.

As a result, functions are ideal for handling and changing this kind of data.

Changes often occur to produce outcomes, such as discovering results. And the set of instructions needed to do this comes from logically sound code blocks that can be used more than once.

A function is a primary code. It's necessary since every other function is linked to it and runs from your main code.

But, if the function has not yet been created, you must first define it before using it. The stages of a function's execution are outlined in its definition.

Consider this: is it preferable to write a code snippet ten times or to write it once and run it ten times?

As a result, functions are just actions that a user wants to do.

But if you declare a function once and give it a name, you can use it more than once without making your main programs look scary. This often reduces the number of lines of code and even simplifies debugging.

We'll get to it later, but for now, you should realize why you need to utilize function is because of the feature of reusability. Since sophisticated procedures may be bundled into single activities that can be performed with a single call by its name, computer programs have become more visible.

Nowadays, every computer programming language enables you to build and utilize these functions to fulfill several tasks with a single call. You may even call it an unlimited number of times without having to bother about logically arranging its code into your main code each time.

Now, consider the following scenario: Imagine you have a television that can hold a large number of channels, receive digital radio broadcasts, convert them into what we view, and provide us with extra choices for other functions.

Yet, this does not suggest that there is a person intelligently programming the lines of code for what you view every time you turn on your television.

Instead, functions for each activity in its operation have been appropriately defined once and are often reused depending on the characteristics you seek to employ.

This is accomplished by calling several functions as many times as feasible from the primary feature that is active. As a result, whether you increase or decrease the volume, its declared function is called frequently.

When you have a system executing the main code, you may continue using these functions as required, which simplifies design and innovation.

The important thing to remember is that every time this function is invoked, it does its job in accordance with the instructions provided.

It is how machines learn new functions. The most popular example is a calculator. It has addition, multiplication, division, and other properties. All of these functions are preset in it, but it only completes those that you choose to call by hitting the appropriate button.

Programmers use functions to reduce the time they spend coding and debugging, hence lowering overall development time.

Let's take a closer look at Python functions.

So, what exactly are Python functions?

What would your answer be if someone asked you this question?

Python functions are a fantastic illustration of the reusability characteristic. Therefore, the Python interpreter provides built-in functions that may be used to service a wide variety of applications, from GUI and mathematical computation to web development and testing.

You may also add additional libraries or modules to your application that include pre-defined functions.

All you'll need to do is download the relevant packages depending on their documentation and then import them into your code to get access to all of their crucial features.

As a result, once declared, a function may be utilized at any time and in any location in your code. Python adheres to the DRY concept of software patterns or codes that include abstractions to reduce repetition and ensure they may be utilized freely without disclosing any underlying components of their implementations.

The entire meaning of DRY is Don't Repeat Yourself, and having reusable pieces of code is important for attaining abstraction in Python. To utilize a function, all you need is its name, parameters, purpose, and the kind of results it returns if it does.

It's nearly like using a telephone, where you don't need to understand how its components function to utilize them. Instead, they've been designed to perform conventional operations that you may use directly to achieve your aims while devoting your time to implementing all of your application program's new features. And no one cares how a function in your software works on the inside as long as it fulfills the job.

Hence, unless you wish to develop or alter an existing function, you shouldn't be concerned with what occurs within the function in Python.

A function is a short program that processes input and produces output.

To utilize a function, you must first define it. In Python, functions are defined by using the def keyword before the name of the function, followed by parentheses and a colon.

Types of Functions in Python

Python functions are classified into three types.

- Built-in functions such as min () for determining the minimal value and print () for displaying an object to the Python terminal are available.

- User-defined functions are functions that users may create and utilize.

- Anonymous functions are available. Since they are not defined with the conventional def keyword, these functions are sometimes known as lambda functions.

Functions vs. Methods

A method is an example of a class-specific function. A method may be accessed by utilizing a class instance. But, functions are not restricted in this way. It just indicates a one-stop function.

This implies that although all methods are functions, not all functions are methods.

Consider the following example. The function plus () is defined, as well as a class of sum ().

```
# Define a function `plus()`
def plus(a,b):
return a + b
# Create a `Summation` class
class Summation(object):
```

def sum(self, a, b):

self.contents = a + b

return self.contents

Hence, in order to invoke the function sum (), you must first define an instance of the object class. Now, let's get started on defining this object:

To use'sum(),' instantiate the 'Summation' class.

Summation() sumInstance = sumInstance.

sum(1,2)

Take in mind that the above instantiation is irrelevant when using thc addition () method. Yet, you may do the addition (1,2) without incident.

Arguments vs parameters

Parameters are names that are used when defining a function and into which parameters will be contained. This signifies that arguments are components of the function.

The sum () method had two arguments in the previous example, despite the fact that the class had three parameters, self, a, and b.

Every class method's first parameter refers to the current class instance. Summation is used in the preceding example.

As a result, referencing self is impossible since self is the parameter name for an implicitly given argument that refers to the instance method being executed.

Defining User Functions

When defining Python functions, the four phases are as follows:

1. First, type the def keyword, followed by the name of the function.

2. Provide the function parameters. The arguments must be enclosed by the function's parentheses. A colon should be used to end the line.

3. Provide statements that the functions must follow.

4. Provide a return statement.

Example:

```
def hello():
print("Hello World")
return
```

Don't forget that your user-created functions may have one or more function arguments.

Return Statement

```
def hello():

print("Hello World")

return("hello")

def hello_noreturn():

print("Hello World")

# Multiply the output of `hello()` with 2

hello() * 2

# (Try to) multiply the output of

`hello_noreturn()` with 2

hello_noreturn() * 2
```

The second function throws an error because working on a None value is impossible. As a result, if you execute this code, you will get a TypeError indicating that you cannot finish the multiplication operation using NoneType.

When a function encounters a return statement, it instantly terminates.

```python
def run():

for x in range(10):

if x == 2:

return

print("Run!")

run()
```

A return statement may show several values. Tuples enable you to return multiple statements.

Look at the following example to see how you may return several values.

```python
# Define `plus()`

def plus(a,b):

sum = a + b

return (sum, a)

# Call `plus()` and unpack variables
```

sum, a = plus(3,4)

Print `sum()`

print(sum)

Calling a Function

You learned how to invoke a function in the previous examples. As the name implies, calling a function means executing the process either straight from the Python prompt or from another function.

You invoke your hello () function by typing hello ().

Adding Docstring to a Python Function

The docstring is the most important aspect of designing Python functions.

The documentation string

Docstrings are another important aspect of writing Python functions. Docstrings define the duties performed by your functions, such as their return values.

The descriptions serve as documentation for your function. Anyone can understand the docstring without having to look at all of the code in the function declaration.

The function docstrings are surrounded in triple quotation marks and come immediately after the function header. The appropriate Docstring for the hello () function is "Hello World."

```python
def hello():
    """Prints "Hello World".

    Returns:
        None
    """
    print("Hello World")
    return
```

Note that docstring might have more than one value.

If you want to learn more about docstrings, go to the Github repositories of Python libraries, where you'll find plenty of examples.

Python Function Arguments

You learned the distinction between arguments and parameters from the outset. In a nutshell, arguments are items that are sent to any function or method call, while the function or method code refers to the arguments by their parameter names. Python user-defined functions may take one of four types of arguments:

- Keyword arguments

- Default arguments

- Required arguments

- Variable number of arguments.

Keyword Arguments

Keyword Arguments Include the keyword arguments # in your function call if you wish to call the parameters in the right order. Example: #

#Define `plus()` function

def plus(a,b):

return a + b

Call `plus()` function with parameters

plus(2,3)

Call `plus()` function with keyword arguments

plus(a=1, b=2)

You may also use the keyword arguments to change the order of the parameters and still get the same result when you execute your function.

```
# Define `plus()` function
def plus(a,b):
return a + b
# Call `plus()` function with keyword arguments
plus(b=2, a=1)
```

Required Arguments

These are arguments that must be present, as the name implies. These parameters must be given during the function call and in the precise sequence shown in the example below:

```
# Define 'plus ()' with the necessary parameters.
```

```
def plus(a,b):

return a + b
```

Global and Local Variables

Variables declared inside a function's body have global scope. In other words, local variables are declared inside a function block and can only be used inside that function. Global variables, on the other hand, can be accessed by any function in your script.

```
# Global variable `init`

init = 1

# Define `plus()` function to accept a variable

number of arguments

def plus(*args):

# Local variable `sum()`

total = 0

for i in args:
```

```
total += i

return total

# Access the global variable

print("this is the initialized value " + str(init))

# (Try to) access the local variable

print("this is the sum " + str(total))
```

When you try to display the local variable total that was declared inside the function body, you will get a NameError indicating that the name 'total' is not defined. On the other hand, the init variable may be shown without difficulty.

Anonymous Functions within Python

Anonymous functions are sometimes known as lambda functions since they make use of lambda. Example:

```
double = lambda x: x*2
```

double(5)

This function is different from the other examples in the first part of this chapter in that it doesn't have a name. When you need an unknown function for a brief period of time, you utilize lambda functions. Particular scenarios where this may be significant are filter (), map (), and reduce ():

reduce import from functools

```
my_list = [1,2,3,4,5,6,7,8,9,10]
# Use lambda function with `filter()`
filtered_list = list(filter(lambda x: (x*2 > 10),
my_list))
# Use lambda function with `map()`
mapped_list = list(map(lambda x: x*2, my_list))
# Use lambda function with `reduce()`
reduced_list = reduce(lambda x, y: x+y, my_list)
```

```
print(filtered_list)

print(mapped_list)

print(reduced_list)
```

The Main () Function

If you've ever coded in another language, like Java, you'll know that the main function is required to execute functions. As seen in the preceding example, this function is not required in Python.

But, if your Python program has a main () function, it might be useful to structure your code logically.

It's simple to create and call a main () function in the same manner you've done with previous functions.

```
# Define `main()` function
```

```
def main():

hello()

print("This is a main function")

main()
```

Presently, when you import it as a module, the code of your main () function will be called. To prevent this, execute the main () function when _ _ name_ _ = '_ _ main_ _'

Apart from the _ _ main_ _ function, there is also the _ _ init_ _ function, which is used to initialize a class or object instance. This is a constructor, and it is called every time a new instance of a class is made. The newly constructed object is assigned to the argument self-using that function.

Chapter 6: Python Operators

```
504          if not hasattr(self, '_headers_buffer'):
505              self._headers_buffer = []
506          self._headers_buffer.append(("%s %d %s\r\n" %
507                  (self.protocol_version, code, message)).encode(
508                      'latin-1', 'strict'))
509
510      def send_header(self, keyword, value):
511          """Send a MIME header to the headers buffer."""
512          if self.request_version != 'HTTP/0.9':
513              if not hasattr(self, '_headers_buffer'):
514                  self._headers_buffer = []
515              self._headers_buffer.append(
516                  ("%s: %s\r\n" % (keyword, value)).encode('latin-1', 'strict'))
517
518          if keyword.lower() == 'connection':
519              if value.lower() == 'close':
520                  self.close_connection = True
521              elif value.lower() == 'keep-alive':
522                  self.close_connection = False
```

Python operators are used to performing operations on values and variables. Operators have the ability to change individual components and output results. The data pieces are referred to as operands. Keywords or distinctive characters are both used to express operators.

Arithmetic operators

They do various arithmetic operations such as subtraction, division, addition, exponentiation, and so on. You can do math calculations in Python in a number of ways, such as by defining variables or calling functions.

Consider a basic example of addition where you add two-digit 2+3=5 to the arithmetic operators.

```
b= 4
c= 5
print (b + c)
```

You may still utilize mathematical operations like division, subtraction, and multiplication.

Python logical operators

Python has three logical operators.

or, and, not As an example:

a or b

a and b

not a

not b

Operator precedence

A set of priorities determines the operators in Python. The table below displays the operator precedence in Python.

	Description	Operators
1	Exponentiation	**
2	Ccomplement, unary plus, and minus	~, +, -
3	Multiplication, division, modulo, and floor division	*, /, %, //
4	addition and subtraction	+ -
5	Right and left bitwise shift	>>, <<
6	Bitwise 'AND'	&
7	Regular `OR' and Bitwise exclusive 'OR'	|, ^
8	Comparison operators	<= < > >=
9	Equality operators	== !=
10	Assignment operators	=, +=, -=, *-, /=, %= //= **=
11	Identity operators	is, is not
12	Membership operators	in, not in
13	Logical operators	or, and, not

Chapter 7: File Handling

Python has a crucial functionality for reading data from and writing data to files.

Most computer languages store all values or data in volatile variables.

Since data is only kept in such variables at run-time and will vanish after the program execution stops, it is preferable to keep this data permanently utilizing files.

When you save data to a file, the next step is to get it back since it is stored as bits of 1s and 0s. If the retrieval fails, the data is no longer usable and is said to be corrupted.

How Python Handles Files?

If you're working on a large software program that processes a large quantity of data, we can't expect the data to be stored in a variable since variables are volatile.

As a result, while dealing with these scenarios, the function of files will come into play.

Since files are non-volatile, the data will be stored permanently on a secondary device such as a hard disk, and you may use Python to interact with these files in your applications.

Do You Consider How Python Will Handle These Files?

Assume that ordinary people will deal with these files. If you wish to read data from a file or put data into a file, you must first open the file or create a new file if the file does not already exist, then do the standard read/write operations, save the file, then close it.

Similarly, the same tasks are carried out in Python using built-in apps.

Types of Files in Python

Files are classified into two types:

1. Text documents

2. Binary data files

A text file is a file whose contents may be viewed using a text editor. A text file is a collection of ASCII characters.

Text files include Python applications.

A binary file stores data in the same way as memory does. Examples of binary files are mp3 files and word documents. A binary file cannot be viewed using a text editor.

The following are the stages involved in file processing in Python.

- Open a file and return the filehandle.
- To read or write an action, use the handle.
- Finish closing the filehandle.

Before you can read or write to a file in Python, you must first open it. After the read/write transaction is complete, you should end it to release the resources associated with the file.

Let's take a closer look at each stage.

Access mode: This is represented as a number, for example, read, write, and add. The read-only r> is the default configuration.

Buffering: The default buffering value is 0. A 0 value indicates that buffering will not occur. If the value is 1, line buffering will take place when accessing the file. If it is more than one, the buffering action will be performed dependent on the size.

File name: A string representing the name of the file to which you wish to get access.

File open modes in Python language

<r>

<rb+>

<rb>

<w+>

<wb+>

<r+>

<w>

<wb>

Python File Object Properties

When you use the Python open () method, an object called the filehandle is returned. You should also be aware that Python files vary in their functionality. You can also use the filehandle to list the characteristics of a file to which it belongs.

Close a File in Python

After you complete your work, always shut the file. Python, on the other hand, features a garbage collector that cleans away unneeded objects.

Nevertheless, it would help if you accomplished it on your own rather than delegating it to the GC.

The Close Method

To close a file, Python provides the close ()> function.

When you close a file, the system allocates resources to it.

And it's not difficult to do.

Closing a file frees up valuable system resources. If you forget to shut the file, Python will do it for you after the program finishes or the file object is no longer referenced inside the program.

But, if your software is huge and you are reading or writing several files, this might require a considerable amount of system resources. You may run out of resources if you continue to open

new files irresponsibly.

Chapter 8: Dictionaries

This chapter will teach you about a new data structure called the dictionary. The dictionary (also known as a hashtable or hashmap in other languages) is one of Python's most sophisticated data structures. Fortunately, since it is integrated into the Python language, you do not need to implement it yourself. You will also be introduced to tuples. What you will discover:

· Using a Dictionary Data Structure

· How to Apply Tuples

Understanding the Python dictionary can help you represent many real-world items more precisely. You will design a dictionary describing a person and store as much information about the individual as you like. You may save their location, personal information, career, and any other characteristics you want to mention. You'll be able to save any two types of information that may be compared, such as a list of terms and their definitions.

In Python, a dictionary contains key-value pairs. Each key is associated with a value, and you may use that key to get the value associated with that key.

A key's value might be a string, an integer, or even another dictionary. In fact, every object that you can create in Python may be used as a value in a dictionary.

Python dictionaries are enclosed by braces, which contain a sequence of key-value pairs.

A key-value pair is a set of values that are tied to each other.

When you give Python a key, it will return the value associated with that key.

The most basic dictionary example contains only one key-value combination.

Example:

'alien' ='color':'green'

This dictionary only has one piece of information about aliens: their color. This dictionary's key is the string 'color,' which is linked to the value 'green.'

Getting Setup

In this part, you will use the Python Idle editor as well as the terminal. With the Idle editor, you will learn about the dictionary before going on to building your own files and interacting with data.

How to Access the Values Inside a Dictionary?

To get the value associated with a key, enter the dictionary's name and the key within square brackets, as illustrated below:

print(alien['color'])

This function returns the value associated with the dictionary key 'color'.

Inside a dictionary, there may be an infinite number of key-value pairs.

Adding New Key-value Pairs

Dictionaries evolve all the time, and you may add new key-value pairs to them at any moment. For example, to add a new key-value pair put the name of the dictionary followed by the new key in square brackets.

We wish to add two types of information to the alien lexicon right now:

It is the x and y coordinates of the extraterrestrial. These coordinates will enable you to place the alien on the screen in a precise location. Place the alien on the left edge of the screen. This will be 25 pixels from top to bottom. Since screen coordinates begin in the upper-left corner, you will place the alien on the left side of the screen by setting the x-coordinate to 0 and 25 pixels from the top by setting the y-coordinate to positive 25, as illustrated below:

```
alien = {'color': 'green', 'points': 5}
print(alien)
u alien['x_position'] = 0
v alien['y_position'] = 25
print(alien)
```

We start by defining the same dictionary we've been using. Then, print this dictionary and present a summary of its contents.

You add a new key-value pair to the dictionary in the second line:

```
{'color': 'green', 'points': 5}
{'color': 'green', 'points': 5, 'y_position': 25, 'x_position': 0}
```

The final dictionary version has four key-pair values.

Note that Python does not care about the sequence of storage; it simply manages the relationship between each key and its value.

The Second Major Data Structure – The Dictionary

The Dictionary is a strong data structure with a 'key' and a 'value'. Each key in the dictionary is distinct and has a corresponding value. The linked value, on the other hand, does not have to be unique.

Real-world examples of dictionaries include:

o A telephone directory:

o Crucial - The phone number

o Value - The individual's name

o A physical dictionary (from which this data structure gets its name)

o Crucial - The term

o Value - The word's definition (i.e., the definition).

o A university student identification number

o Key - the number

o Value - The individual's name

o Your Subway Rewards Card:

o Key - Your credit card number

o Value - The number of points you've earned!

In the dictionary, the key might be a string or a number. In fact, any data type may be used! The message is that the key must be one-of-a-kind!

Here are some sample tables from the preceding examples to demonstrate keys and values once more.

Key(Phone number)

    Value(Persons name)

7323245	'Joe'
9822912	'Sue'
6323421	'Moe

It is worth noting that the phone number is represented as an integer, and each of the values is expressed as a string.

Key(Word)

    Value(Definition)

'Cat'
'A small domesticated carnivore'

'Python'
Any of several boa constrictors in the subfamily Pythoninae'

'Byte'
Adjacent bits, usually eight, proce ssed by a computer as a unit

In this example, the key is a string, and the value is likewise a string.

Key (Student ID Number).

Value (Persons Name)

127323

'Mike'

187428

'Tomoki'

493209

'Raoul'

Key (Reward Card Number).

Value (Points)

1209482104812	47
2098520935820	434
3248098324093	434

It's important to note that the points in this example could be different, and dictionaries let us change them. Values can be copied, but keys can't (if there are two keys with the same name, the older one will be used).

About Learning to Program: A dictionary is one of several data structures built into Python that we may use. In reality, we always have a huge number of other data structures and algorithms available to us. It might even become frightening or overpowering! Still, I think you should do this exercise (and the ones that come after it) at least once, even if you don't understand everything. Then go through the specifics again. The greatest method to learn is frequently to finish a project and then revisit it with a better understanding of what issue you are attempting to address and what is vital to study and grasp in great depth.

Dictionary Examples

To model a phonebook, first develop a dictionary. The first step is to select whether our key will be a name or a value.

You may use a phone number, as seen in the preceding example.

Since phone numbers are unique, they are a suitable option for a key.

Yet, since it is simpler for us to remember someone's name, you may also use it as a key.

'Mike' phoneBook: 55555555 # The important word is 'Mike.'

You can only have one buddy called Mike in this scenario. If you want additional Mikes, you must save them as Mike01, Mike02, Mike03, and so on.

You may print a particular phonebook record by doing the following:

phoneBook['Mike'] print

To make a copy of the whole phonebook, you can just use the print command.

Print phoneBook

print phonebook

You'll want to expand and edit your vocabulary over time, so you may add words like the ones below.

Add a new item
phoneBook['Michelle'] = 43255322

Lets confirm our entry went in.

print phonebook

Delete Mike from our phonebook, we'll never need to call him!

del phoneBook['Mike']

```
# If Michelle changes her number, we can update it by accessing
her
entry with her key ('Michelle') and then simply re-assigning a new
value.
phoneBook['Michelle'] = 3252352


# Confirm our changes have been made.
print phonebook


# Sometimes we are not sure who is in our phonebook, so we have
to
# iterate over all of # the keys. When we know what keys are
available,
```

```
# we can then use those keys to quickly index
into our phone book
and
# retrieve the value (a phone number in this
case).
# print keys
for x in phoneBook:
print x
# Alternatively, if we just need the numbers, we
can print out all of
the values.
# This might be a nice thing to do if you want to
call everyone and
wish them a happy
# new year.

# This might be an evil thing to do if you want to
call everyone and
```

try to scam them!

Look out!

print values

for x in phoneBook:

print phoneBook[x]

ANOTHER LOOK AT THE DICTIONARY

The dictionary is an 'associative data structure,' as the name implies.

This signifies that a value is linked to a key. It makes complete sense! This should be obvious since this is often how our brain operates. We don't usually think of a number and say, well, that's Mike's number. We usually think of a name (for example, 'Mike' and then recollect his phone number. Associating one thing with another is a key part of how our brains work, so it shouldn't be a surprise that we can do the same with computers.

THE TUPLE

In Python, the Tuple is a technique to combine information together. It's similar to a list; only we can't change it after we've made a tuple.

Let's make a tuple that contains information on a certain individual.

Let's make a Human Tuple that accepts str and an int as the two sorts of data to store. The first element is a string containing a name, and the second is an integer containing the number of miles they ran this month.

```
Person = ('Mike',100)
>>> Person
('Mike', 100)
```

As a result, the tuple is just a collection of values kept together. We can actually store tuples in a list if we wish. Let's make some additional tuples with names and the value of each person's preferred number in a second field.

```
>>> Mike = ('Mike',1)
>>> Willie = ('Willie',2)
>>> Tomoki = ('Tomoki', 17)
>>> Raoul = ('Raoul',14)
>>> BestFriends = [Willie,Mike,Tomoki,Raoul]
>>> BestFriends
[('Willie', 2), ('Mike', 1), ('Tomoki', 17), ('Raoul', 14)]
```

When we produce the BestFriends list, we can see that each element (separated by a comma) is a tuple that we constructed. We may then retrieve items in our list by using their position in the list, just as we did before. Now our list will yield a tuple. When we look at the type of entry, we discover that it is, indeed, a tuple.

```
>>> BestFriends[0]
('Willie', 2)
>>> type(BestFriends[0])
<type 'tuple'>
```

This may take some getting accustomed to since we're utilizing two layers of indirection to get to the specific piece we want. Yet, with enough experience, you will be able to perform this with ease. Let's put everything we've learned about dictionaries and tuples together. Let's put up the...NBA Superstar Basketball Dictionary!

CHALLENGE PROBLEM

Take the NBA player data below and build tuples for them. The format is as follows:

The number of championships won is the first value in the tuple, while the number of seasons played is the second.

Key

Value

Bill Russel

(11,13)

Sam Jones

(10,12)

Robert Horry

(7,16)

Michael Jordan

(6,15)

Shaquille O'Neil

(4,19)

Mike Shah

(0,0)

Example:

Creating a tuple.

samJones = (10,12)

As a result, the variable'samJones' has the tuple (10,12).

Then, we'd want to put all of these players (or, more accurately, their "tuples") into a dictionary and get a list of all NBA players who have won at least one championship.

Here's an example of how to create an empty dictionary and then add our player to it.

Now let's create an empty dictionary

nbaDictionary = {}

Add a key of 'Sam Jones' and a

value of samJones (which is a tuple)

nbaDictionary['Sam Jones'] = samJones

Goals:

· Output all NBA players in our vocabulary who have won at least one title.

· Return all NBA players in our vocabulary who has won a championship in at least 50% of their seasons.

Hints and gotchas:

· After entering your entries, print out your dictionary to view the data graphically.

· In mathematics, can we divide by zero?

· To compare two conditions, use a 'and' phrase.

o For example, if value > 5 and value!= 0:

· When we divide two numbers, we receive back one integer. We must divide into floats if we want a float (decimal number) as a result.

o As an example:

```
>>> 7/5
1
>>> float(7)/float(5)
1.4
```

Chapter 9: Object-Oriented Programming

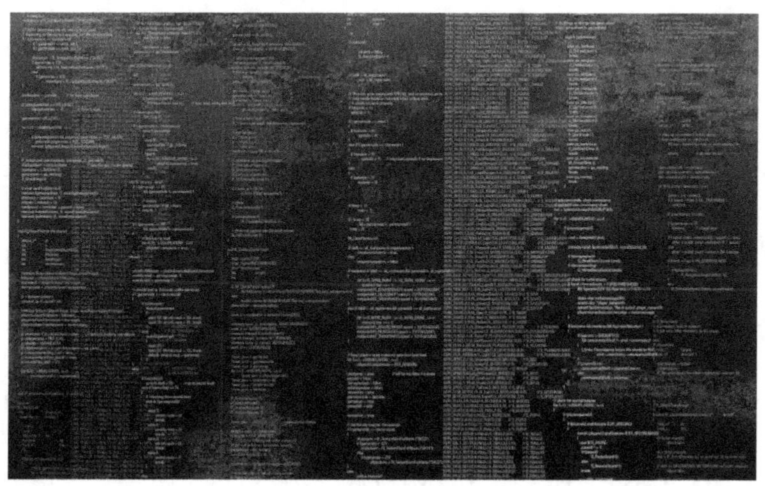

Object-Oriented programming is a broad idea that is used to build sophisticated programs. Data scientists must, among other things, create apps to deal with data. This chapter will go through the fundamentals of object-oriented programming in Python.

OOP, or Object-Oriented Programming, provides various benefits over other design patterns. The development process is quicker and less expensive, with excellent software maintainability. This, in turn, leads to better software that is also rich in new features and methodologies. The learning curve, on the other hand, is complicated. For newcomers, the concept may be confusing. Since more lines of code have been created, OOP is slower and requires more memory in terms of calculation.

Object-oriented programming is based on the idea that you can change the state of a program with statements. It focuses on demonstrating how software should work.

Imperative programming languages include Java, C++, C, Ruby, and Python. This differs from declarative programming, which deals with what a computer program should do without specifying how. Database query languages such as XQuery and SQL are examples.

The property of classes and objects is essential to OOP. A class may be thought of as a "blueprint" for things. They may have their own distinct properties and execution techniques.

Example of OOP

Consider the class Dog as an example. Don't think of it in terms of a particular dog or your own dog. We're talking about what a dog is and what it can do. Dogs have ages and names. These are attributes of instances. Barking is a tactic used by dogs.

In programming, when you talk about a specific dog, you have an object: an object is a class instance. This is the actual state upon which object-oriented programming is based.

Let's have a look at OOP in Python.

Python is a strong programming language that supports object-oriented programming. You will use Python to create a class with attributes and methods that you will later call. Python offers advantages over other languages. First and foremost, the language is dynamic and uses a high-level data type. This means that development is quicker than in Java. The programmer is not required to define variable types and arguments. Python is, therefore, simple to learn for novices. Its code is more user-friendly and readable.

It is critical to realize that a class essentially gives structure. This is a blueprint that specifies how something should be defined. It does not, however, provide any substantial material. For example, the shape () class tells you how big a shape is and what it's called, but it doesn't tell you what a form's name is.

A class may be thought of as an idea for how something should be done.

Python Objects

Even though the class is the blueprint, objects or instances are members of a certain class. It's no longer a notion. It's a simple form, like a three-sided triangle.

A class is analogous to a questionnaire. It will provide the necessary details. After you finish the form, your real copy becomes an instance of the class. It contains unique information that is important to you.

You can make a lot of copies to have a lot of copies, but if you don't have the form, you won't know what information is needed. So, before you can make an instance of a class, you must first explain what the class needs.

Defining a Class in Python

A basic Python class definition follows:

Class Dog (object)

Pass

When creating a class in Python, you start with the class keyword to indicate that you're writing a class, and then you follow it with the class name. The name of the class in the preceding example is Dog.

The Python keyword pass is used in the above class description as a placeholder where code would eventually go. This keyword was used to prevent the code from throwing an error.

The parentheses around the object section show that you are inheriting from the parent class. But since this is the implicit default in Python 3, this is no longer necessary.

Objects Attributes

Every class defines an object, and every object has properties known as attributes. The _init_ () function is used to describe the default value of an object's initial properties. This method takes at least one parameter, which is the self-variable that describes the object.

```
class Dog:

    # Initializer / Instance Attributes
    def __init__(self, name, age):
        self.name = name
        self.age = age
```

In the following example, each dog has a different name and age, which is essential to understand, particularly when attempting to distinguish various breeds. Remember that the class simply defines the Dog and does not create objects of individual dogs with unique names and ages.

Similarly, the self-variable is associated with a class instance.

Since each class instance has a unique value, you may write Dog.

Instead of self, user name.

The name is the same as the name.

Class Attributes

Although instance attributes are unique to each object, class characteristics are shared by all instances. All dogs in this situation.

Methods

When you have attributes belonging to a class, you may construct functions to access the class attribute. Methods are the names given to these functions. When declaring methods, you should use a selfkeyword to supply the method's initial parameter.

For example, you might create a class Snake that has the attribute name and the function change name. The method change name will take a new name parameter as well as the keyword self.

You may now instantiate this class with a variable snake and modify the name using the change name function.

```
>>> # instantiate the class
>>> snake = Snake()

>>> # print the current object name
>>> print(snake.name)
python

>>> # change the name using the change_name method
>>> snake.change_name("anaconda")
>>> print(snake.name)
anaconda
```

Instance Attributes and the init Method

During runtime, you may still supply values for the attributes. The attributes are defined inside the init method. Consider the following example:

```
class Snake:

    def __init__(self, name):
        self.name = name

    def change_name(self, new_name):
        self.name = new_name
```

You may now continue to specify various attribute values for distinct objects directly.

Thus far, you've learned how to create Python classes and methods, instantiate objects and invoke instance methods. These abilities will come in handy while dealing with difficult challenges.

If you use object-oriented programming, your code will get more complicated as the size of your program grows. There will be several classes, objects, instance methods, and subclasses. You'll want to keep your code up-to-date and readable. You will need to follow design patterns to do this. These are guidelines that may help you avoid terrible design. Each symbolizes a specific program that always appears in OOP and describes the solution to that problem, which can subsequently be utilized again.

Chapter 10: Inheritance

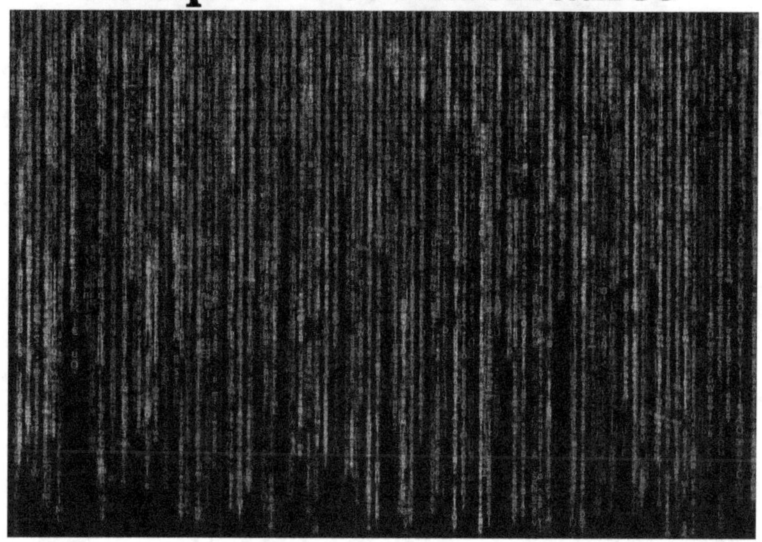

We often come across things that have a basic version and an advanced version that has more features than the basic version. An OOP software modeling technique lets you build a new class by adding more features to an existing class instead of starting from scratch. In OOP language, this is known as an inheritance; the existence of a class is known as the parent or base class, and the new class is known as the child or subclass.

When a new class has the 'IS A' connection with an existing class, inheritance is involved.

Dogs ARE animals. A cat is also an animal. As a result, the base class is an animal, whereas the inherited classes are a dog and a cat.

A quadrilateral is a shape with four sides. A rectangle, like a square, is a quadrilateral. A quadrilateral is a base class (also known as a parent class), while rectangle and square are inherited classes (also known as child classes).

The parent class's data definitions and methods are passed down to the child class. This makes it easier to utilize previously accessible features. The child class may add a few different definitions or redefine a method from the base class.

This feature is especially helpful for putting things in a system into a class hierarchy. It is also feasible to create a new class that is built on many existing classes. This is known as multiple inheritances.

The following diagram depicts the general method of inheritance:

Syntax:

class parent:

statements

class child(parent):

statements

The name of the parent class is placed in parenthesis in front of the name of the child class to indicate the relationship between the two.

The object of the child class will take on the instance properties and methods of the parent class.

To make an example easier to understand, build a quadrilateral class first. This class is then used as a base class for the rectangle class.

This code sets up a quadrilateral class with four sides as instance variables and a perimeter () method:

```python
class quadrilateral:
    def __init__(self, a, b, c, d):
        self.side1=a
        self.side2=b
        self.side3=c
        self.side4=d

    def perimeter(self):
        p=self.side1 + self.side2 + self.side3 + self.side4
        print("perimeter=",p)
```

The constructor (the __init__() function) is given four arguments, which are then assigned to four instance variables. Declare the aforementioned class's object and use the perimeter() function to put it to the test.

```
>>>q1=quadriLateral(7,5,6,4)
>>>q1.perimeter()
perimeter=22
```

We now create a rectangle class based on the quadriLateral class (a quadrilateral IS a rectangle!). It should be able to use the instance variables and perimeter() function from the base class without having to change it.

Since the opposing sides of the rectangle are identical, we only need two adjacent sides to build its object. As a result, the __init__() method's other two arguments are set to none.

Using the super() function, the __init__() method passes the arguments to the constructor of its base (quadrilateral) class. Sides 3 and 4 are set to none when the object is created. The constructor of the rectangle class makes opposite sides equal. Recall that the perimeter() function was immediately inherited. As a result, there is no need to redefine it.

Inheritance class rectangle(quadriLateral) example:

```
def __init__(self, a, b):
super().__init__(a, b, a, b)
```

We can now define the rectangle class object and utilize the perimeter() function.

```
>>> r1=rectangle(10, 20)
>>> r1.perimeter()
perimeter=60
```

Overriding in Python

In the above example, we can see how base class resources are utilized while generating the inherited class. The inherited class, on the other hand, may have its own instance properties and methods.

Methods from the parent class may be used in the inherited class. But, we may change the functionality of any base class method if necessary. To that end, the inherited class includes a new definition of a method (with the same name and signature as the base class). Clearly, the object of a new class will have access to both methods, but when called, the one from its own class will take priority. This is known as method overriding.

Then, we'll create a new function in the rectangle class called area() and utilize it as the foundation for the square class. The rectangle's area is the product of its neighboring sides.

Example:

```
class rectangle(QuadriLateral):
def __init__(self, a,b):
super().__init__(a, b, a, b)
def area(self):
a = self.side1 * self.side2
print("area of rectangle=", a)
```

Let us define the square class, which is a descendant of the rectangle class.

The area() function is overridden in order to implement the formula for the square area as the square of its sides.

Example:

```python
class square(rectangle):

def __init__(self, a):

super().__init__(a, a)

def area(self):

a=pow(self.side1, 2)

print('Area of Square: ', a)

>>>s=Square(10)

>>>s.area()

Area of Square: 100
```

Chapter 11: Introduction to Django Framework

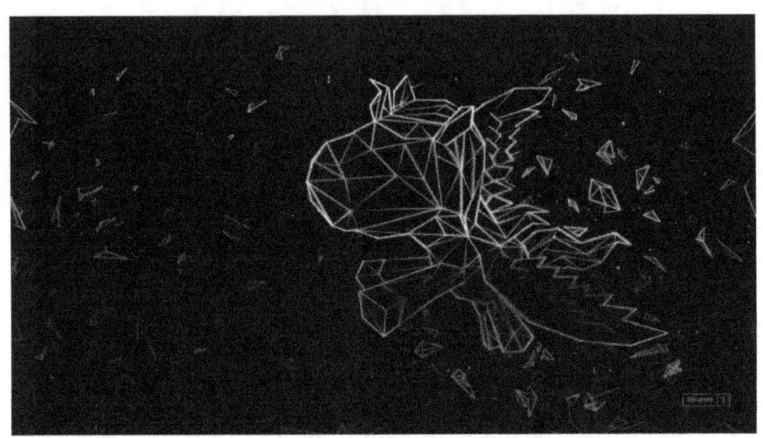

Django is one of the most advanced Python web frameworks for building and maintaining websites quickly.

Most of the pros and cons of web development are taken care of by the Django framework, so you can focus on building your app without having to start from scratch. Django is open source and free, with an active community and excellent documentation.

Django will assist you in developing software that is:

• **Complete**

Django follows the "batteries included" principle and has almost everything a developer could want. Because everything you need is included in the one-stop shop, it works seamlessly together, adheres to a consistent design principle, and has up-to-date documentation.

• **Scalable**

Django uses a component-based "shared-nothing" format that can be substituted or changed as needed. There are clear differences between the different parts, which means that it can be made to handle more traffic by adding hardware at any level. Some of the most popular websites have successfully scaled Django to meet their needs.

- **Versatile**

You can use Django to create any website that you want right, from content management systems to social networks and news sites.

This framework can work with any client-side framework and can support content in any format.

- **Easy to maintain**

The Django framework is built based on design principles that make it easy to reuse code. It also allows the grouping of similar functions into reusable applications.

- **Portability**

Django is developed in Python, which runs on multiple platforms. In other words, you're not forced to use a specific server platform alone, but you can run applications on any platform of your choice.

- **It's secure**

Developers have nothing to fear that hackers will steal vital information from their websites or gain entry into their website applications. Django has an excellent security system that automatically protects the website.

Where Did Django Come From?

Django was developed between 2003-2005 by a team of web experts who were responsible for building and managing newspaper websites.

After making several websites, the team started to reuse most of the standard code and design patterns. This common code resulted in a general web development framework.

Since 2005 when it was open-sourced, Django has continued to expand with new releases. Each release brought new functionality and fixed several bugs.

Today, Django is driving the web development environment, with thousands of users going for Django. While it still has some properties that show its past, Django has matured into a powerful framework that can construct any website.

What is the Level of Popularity of Django?

There is no freely accessible scale for measuring the popularity of server-side frameworks. A great question is if Django is capable of dealing with issues on unpopular platforms. Is it still in the works? Can you receive help if you need it? Is it possible for you to acquire a job if you study Django?

Django is a popular framework based on the number of high-profile websites that use it, the number of individuals who contribute to the codebase, and the number of people who provide free and paid assistance.

Is it Opinionated?

Web frameworks are classified as "opinionated" or "unopinionated."

An opinionated framework is one that has strong feelings about the "correct" approach to doing a job. Since the appropriate method to accomplish anything is well-documented and recognized, these frameworks enable rapid development in a certain topic. Even so, they might not be as flexible when it comes to solving problems and tend to offer fewer options for how to do things.

On the other hand, unopinionated frameworks don't tell you how to put pieces together to reach a certain goal or even what pieces should be used. They make it easier for developers to use the best tools to do a specific job.

In one aspect, Django is a little opinionated and hence provides the "best of both worlds". It gives a list of parts that can be used for web development tasks and a suggestion for how to use them. But because Django is not tied to any one option, you can pick and choose between them or add support for new ones if you need to.

Who's Using Django?

It's also a good idea to discover who else is utilizing this framework so you can get an idea of what you can do with it.

Bitbucket, Mozilla, Instagram, National Geographic, Last.fm, and many more well-known websites use Django.

Further examples may be found in the Django sites database, which has a list of over 5000 websites powered by Django.

8 Unique Characteristics of Django

This section will look at Django's distinct features. The characteristics of every technology may explain why it was invented. Every time you learn a new technology, there is a purpose behind it. There are several reasons why you should learn Django. Here's a closer look at Django's distinguishing features and why it's such a strong framework.

In-depth Documentation

If there is an open-source framework with good documentation, Django takes the top spot. Django offers, without question, the greatest documentation on the market.

Documentation is essential for each developer. This is similar to a well-documented library where you can look for anything and determine if it is a syntax or a function.

Once again, one of the greatest qualities of grading technology is its documentation. As a result, it enables other developers besides its inventors to optimize the technology.

From the time it was declared open source to the present, Django has been a pioneer in driving the finest documentation. In reality, documentation has only gotten better as technology has grown, and it is also available in many languages.

2. SEO Optimized

This is an outstanding feature of Django that sets it apart from the competition. Search engine optimization is the technique of increasing the visibility of your website in search engines. When people search for Django, it shows at the top of the results. Search engines depend on an algorithm that may not always agree with the creator. Yet, since the website is designed for people to read and comprehend, as well as the URL from the server.

Django improves on the idea that came before it by keeping the website on the server using URLs instead of IP addresses, which makes it more visible.

3. It's a Python Web-framework

One of the biggest motivators for many individuals to learn Django is that it is a Python framework. Python is a programming language that can tackle any issue. It's plain and simple language. Python is now the most popular programming language on the market. This is due to the fact that it is the easiest language to learn. Python may be used for nearly anything, from web development to machine learning.

These attractive features make Django and Python the most powerful and simple-to-learn frameworks.

To begin programming with Django, you must first have a basic understanding of Python and web development. It promotes rapid growth by being rational and simple.

4. Highly Scalable

Django is used by the majority of MNCs and works well. This is a great illustration of Django's scalability.

The level at which the technology is applied is referred to as scalability. Larger websites, such as Instagram, have a huge number of active users, which generates a significant amount of data. This level necessitates that the program is error-free and precise. Of course, experienced programmers and developers will find it tough.

Expert programmers created Django from the ground up and only used libraries they had created for Python. Django is perfect for anyone who wants to make error-free websites because it has been tested and fixed a lot and has been on the market for a long time.

5. Highly Versatile

Django's nature is adaptable. The logical project structure and Django architecture might look restricting at times. But this is not true because giving us the files gives us a strong base that can be changed into any app we want to build later.

It allows Django integration with all of the technologies we use, as well as new ones. As a consequence, Django has become the property of web development, and everyone who was previously using PHP will mostly use Django.

6. Intensively Tested

While learning new technology, you want it to be solid and resilient enough to withstand the industry's rapid fluctuations. Django, on the other hand, completes that work with zeal.

It is safe to say that Django functions well to handle all traffic and meet international standards because MNCs use it to build projects all over the world.

The framework has been in use for some time, and many flaws and errors have been addressed. So now is the time to begin studying the Django framework. Because of this, the number of web developers who use Django to build websites grows every day.

7. Supports Rapid Development

Although most technologies provide this functionality as the primary feature, Django has many other excellent features.

In this situation, rapid development means that you don't need a lot of back-end knowledge to make a full website. You won't also make separate server files to set up the database and connect it, nor will you make a separate file to move data to and from the server. Django handles this, as well as many other duties. There is no need for new files for each job.

8. Provides Better Security

Django is a very secure programming language. It is a safe language because it automatically checks for bugs, which used to be done by a backend developer. Even though it may be hard to see, experienced backend developers can understand how Django works and how secure it is.

Django's code was written from the ground up, which accounts for its other qualities as well as its security. Since web experts made the framework, you can be sure that most of the problems that web developers face will be taken care of.

Chapter 12: Django Installation

The first step is to install a few apps on your PC so that you can start using Django. Python, Virtualenv, and Django are installed as part of the basic setup.

To summarize:

- You must first install Python.

- The virtual environment that will enable you to isolate your Python and Django applications may then be installed.

- Next, inside the virtual environment, install Django. You may isolate your project in this manner.

Install Python

Installing the most recent Python distribution is the first step.

You can learn how to install Python in earlier chapters, or you can go to www.Python.org and scroll down until you find the download files mentioned.

Choose the appropriate version depending on your Windows distribution. If you're unsure which one is best for you, you may wish to download the Windows x86-64 executable installation version.

Go to your Downloads folder, right-click the installer, and choose Run as administrator.

The next step after installing Python is to locate and launch the Command Prompt software.

Enter the following command to see whether everything is functioning properly:

Python - version

The result should show the Python version that is currently installed on your machine.

If you can see the version of Python installed on your machine, Python is running. Virtual Environments may now be installed.

Installing Virtualenv

Next step, you will use pip to manage and install Python packages. Type the following command into the Command Prompt to install virtualenv.

pip install virtualenv

The installation that has transpired up to this point has been system-wide. Going on everything you install, including Django, will be done inside a Virtual Environment.

Now that you've installed your virtual environment, anything you install from now on will go into a Virtual Environment.

Consider this: before you begin any Django project, you will need to create a virtual environment for it. This is equivalent to building a sandbox for each Django project. So you may mess about it without causing any harm.

After creating your virtual environment, you must activate it before using it.

To activate it, enter the following commands:

venv\Scripts\activate

If you see (venv) in front of the command line, that means it worked. As an illustration:

```
Command Prompt
D:\Users\vitorfs\Development\myproject>venv\Scripts\activate
(venv) D:\Users\vitorfs\Development\myproject>
```

Another important point is that the pip program is already running, and when you use it to install a Python package like Django, it will do so inside the Venv environment.

Then, if you wish to deactivate the venv, run the following command: venvScriptsdeactivate. bat.

So let's keep it turned on for the following several stages.

Django Installation

The installation of Django is simple. Now that the venv is active, enter the command below into the Command Prompt.

Pip install Django

That's all. You are now ready to go. The next step is to launch the Django project. It is now time to construct something.

Starting a New Project

Use the following command to begin a new Django project:

django-admin startproject myproject

When you run the program above, it will construct the fundamental folder structure for a Django project.

Thus far, your myproject directory has the following:

```
myproject/                   <-- higher level folder
 |-- myproject/              <-- django project folder
 |      |-- myproject/
 |      |      |-- __init__.py
 |      |      |-- settings.py
 |      |      |-- urls.py
 |      |      |-- wsgi.py
 |      +-- manage.py
 +-- venv/                   <-- virtual environment folder
```

Django Apps

The Django philosophy contains two main components:

- An app is a web application that does something. An app is made up of models, templates, tests, and views.

- Project: This is a collection of settings and applications. A single project may have numerous applications or a single app.

It's crucial to realize that you can launch a Django app without a project. A basic website, such as a blog, may be powered by a single app called weblog.

Django accepts the idea of an app.

This is a method of organizing the source code. It's not easy to tell what's an app and what isn't at first. How to structure the code, and so forth. So don't worry about it right now! Let's first become acquainted with Django's API and the essentials.

Now, to illustrate, let's create a basic Online Forum Board. To create the initial app, browse to the directory containing the manage.py file and execute the following command:

Django-admin startapp boards

This time, the startapp command is used.

This will give us the directory structure seen below:

```
myproject/
 |-- myproject/
 |    |-- boards/                    <-- our new django app!
 |    |    |-- migrations/
 |    |    |     +-- __init__.py
 |    |    |-- __init__.py
 |    |    |-- admin.py
 |    |    |-- apps.py
 |    |    |-- models.py
 |    |    |-- tests.py
 |    |    +-- views.py
 |    |-- myproject/
 |    |    |-- __init__.py
 |    |    |-- settings.py
 |    |    |-- urls.py
 |    |    |-- wsgi.py
 |    +-- manage.py
 +-- venv/
```

Now that you've built the first app let's set up the project to utilize it.

To do this, visit settings.py and look for the Installed apps variable:

Settings.py

Django already has six built-in applications. These apps offer typical functions that many Web applications need, such as sessions, CSS, static file management, and so on.

In the next chapters, you will learn more about these applications. So for the time being, leave them alone and merely add your boards app to the list of INSTALLED APPS:

Hello, World!

Let's design the first view. In the next chapter, you will learn more about. But for now, let's see how it feels to create a new page in Django.

To begin, open the views.py file in the boards app and add the following code:

```python
from django.http import HttpResponse

def home(request):
    return HttpResponse('Hello, World!')
```

Views are Python functions that take a HttpRequest and return a HttpResponse. Take a request as a parameter and deliver a response as a result. That's the flow you need to remember.

Now, here is a basic view definition called home that returns a message. Hello there, World.

The next step is to tell Django when to provide this view. It occurs in the urls.py file:

Urls.py

```python
from django.conf.urls import url
from django.contrib import admin

from boards import views

urlpatterns = [
    url(r'^$', views.home, name='home'),
    url(r'^admin/', admin.site.urls),
]
```

Chapter 13: MVC Pattern

The preceding part covered installing everything you need. You should now have Python and Django installed. We have generated the project you'll be using.

The MVC Pattern

This section will go through the MVC design pattern. You will have a deeper understanding of the MVC pattern. Django MVC design eliminates numerous difficulties that exist in the conventional web development technique.

Every website on the internet has three key components: input logic, user interface logic, and business logic.

These pieces of code serve many functions, including input logic inside the dataset and data organization in the database.

It just takes input and routes it to the appropriate database. Business logic is the principal controller that handles the server output inside the HTML. As the name implies, the UI logic pertains to the HTML, CSS, and JavaScript pages.

When the conventional method of execution was employed, all of this code was implemented in a single file. This was not a major issue at the time since web pages were mostly static, and websites did not include multimedia or complex code. Moreover, this design causes difficulties for developers during testing and project maintenance.

Today that the times have changed, and websites are becoming bigger and larger on a daily basis while supporting applications such as online artificial intelligence, cloud computing, and online development environments, all of these projects are constructed using the MVC framework.

So, what exactly is MVC? Model View Controller is abbreviated as MVC.

Don't be afraid; you'll study every aspect of the MVC pattern and associate it with Django.

One of the Product Development Architecture patterns is the MVC pattern. It computes the old approach's code challenges in a single file.

The MVC is divided into three sections. This covers the Model, View, and Controller.

The distinction between these components enables the developer to focus on one primary element of the web app and hence write strong code for one function with extensive testing, scalability and debugging.

Let's have a look at the parts:

1. Model

The Model depicts the web-app component that acts as a bridge between the website interface and the database. In technical words, the object performs the logic for the data domain of the application.

Sometimes, the application may merely ingest data from a specific dataset and transmit it straight to the view without needing any database, in which case the dataset is seen as a model.

Nowadays, even if you're developing a basic blog site, you'll need some kind of database if you want to have any kind of website.

Within the Django design, the Model is the component that carries the Business Logic.

For example, when you sign up for a website, you give information to the controller, who then sends it to the models, which include business logic, and store it in the database.

2. View

The Django framework's user interface is found in the View component. HTML, CSS, and other technologies make compose the View. Ultimately, the Interface is built using Model components.

3. Controller

The engine component is the controller. In other words, the controller handles user interaction by clicking a view depending on the model.

The controller's primary role is to choose a view component based on user input and apply the model component.

This architecture has several advantages, which is why Django is based on it. It takes the same model to a more complicated level.

As an illustration:

When the preceding standards are combined, it is evident that the controller is the component that selects various views and transfers data to the model's components.

MTV Pattern

Model-Template-View is abbreviated as MTV. It contains the Templates nomenclature for Views and Views for Controller.

Within the MVC design, templates are linked to the View because they explain the presentation layer, which handles the presentation logic in the framework and determines the material to show and how to deliver it to the user.

Advantages of Using the Django Architecture

The Django framework is built on the design mentioned above, and it interacts across all three components without the need for sophisticated programming. That is why Django is gaining popularity.

Django architecture has many benefits, including:

1. Rapid Development

This Django design separates into several components, making it easier for many developers to work on different parts of the same application at the same time. It is one of Django's characteristics.

2. Loosely Coupled

The Django architecture comprises many sections that rely on each other at various phases of the application, which improves the overall security of the website.

3. Easy to Make Changes

This is a fantastic development feature since the Django architecture is divided into pieces. If there is a change in section parts, you don't need to alter it in other parts.

This is a significant feature of Django since it allows for more website customization than other frameworks.

This section has gone through the Django framework's MVC structure and explained each component in depth. You have also learned several advantages of the Django framework.

Django Project Layout and Different Files Contained in Root Directory

When you create a Django project, the Django framework creates a root directory called the project name. This root directory includes files and folders that provide fundamental functionality to your site, and it is on this solid foundation that you will build your whole website.

Files That Make Up the Django Project Root Directory

The root directory is the location of the manage.py file.

Extra files, such as db.sqlite, are database files that may be accessible when you transfer the project.

The default app that Django offers for you is located in the Django root directory. It includes the files that will be used during the project.

The files in the root directory have important purposes, and once you understand them, Django will make more sense to you. All of these files are in a pretty sensible sequence and are intended for fulfilling particular duties.

Let's begin with the manage.py file:

1. Manage.py

This is the file that contains the project's command line information, and you will use it to launch, debug, and test the project.

The files include code for operating the server, moving the server, and command-line project management.

The preceding file offers all of the features provided by Django-admin, as well as specific project functionalities.

You will often use the following commands when developing your project:

Runserver: This command will start the Django framework's test server. This is another benefit of Django over other frameworks.

Makemigrations: This command is handy for integrating the project files you've contributed to it. This command will simply look for any new contributions to your project and add them to it.

Migrate: The last command includes the migrations you designed in the previous command with the whole project. The difference between this command and the previous one is that the former saves the changes inside the file, whilst the latter apply that modification to the whole project.

2. My_project

This is the project's Python package. It includes the files required to configure the project settings. _init py

This file is empty, and it is there in the project primarily to inform the Python interpreter that the directory listed above is a package. It is one of the standard Python package rules.

Settings.py

The settings.py file is where you will add all apps and middleware applications. This is the primary settings file for the Django project, as the name implies. This file contains information on the installed apps and middleware on this Django project.

It will be added to this file every time you install a new program.

There are several programs that come pre-installed. By default, these apps, such as the Django admin app, give all of the essential functionality you'll ever need for your website.

Urls.py

This file contains information on the project's URLs. The URL stands for universal resource locator, and it displays the address of the resource as well as other components for your website.

The main purpose of this file is to connect the web apps to the project.

This urls.py file will execute anything you type into the URL bar. Afterward, it will associate your request with the app to which you have linked it.

```python
from django.contrib import admin
from django.urls import path

urlpatterns = [
    path('admin/', admin.site.urls),
]
```

The file adds one URL to the admin app by default in the above example. Two parameters may be sent to the path ().

First, the URL is to be searched for in the URL bar on the local server, and then the file you wish to launch when that URL request is matched.

The admin is the pre-made application, and the file is the URL of that app's file. This file serves as a road plan for your Django project.

Wsgi.py

Note that Django is written in Python, which uses the WSGI server for web development. This file handles that, and you won't be utilizing it very often.

Wsgi is still important; however, if you wish to execute the apps on Apache servers or another server since Django is the backend, you will need its compatibility with many servers. But you need not be concerned since each server will get a Django middleware that will handle any connection and integration issues. It would help if you simply had critical and appropriate middleware for your server. It's that easy.

This last part has gone through the Django project structure and how all files in the Django architecture align, and what their function is.

These files are essential and will be accessible in any Django application you create on your own. Its major role is to provide all backend assistance and fix connection issues.

That happens when you're working on the database. It also takes care of the front end and the originality of your website or web application.

Chapter 14: Create, Install, Deploy First Django App

This chapter will teach you how to develop, install, and execute your first Django app. You'll also learn how to add the app to the urls.py file and create the views.py file for the Django project.

Let's get started.

1. Creating a Django App

The key rationale for using web apps is to take advantage of the reusability of the Django code. This will enable you to not only move the project's pre-built apps but also customize online applications.

All commands are accessible in the root directory or the directory containing the manage.py file.

Run this command inside the project directory on your PC before building the Django application.

```
python manage.py makemigrations
```

Run the following command once this command has been completed:

```
python manage.py migrate
```

Creating a Django project is straightforward since you simply need to write a few commands that will be executed on your PC.

In the following example, both terminal and PowerShell users use identical commands:

```
$ django-admin startapp application-name
```

Running these commands will now result in the creation of the application. If you look in the root directory, you'll notice files that the new program will need, and you'll be altering them to achieve your objectives.

Here are some pointers that could be useful:

- Based on the many functions that your apps will do, give them names.

- Create apps only if the job can be completed with a separate application.

If you follow the advice above, you will be able to build modularity in your project. This habit will not only assist you in general practice but will also allow you to be particular about what kind of applications to include in your current project if you construct new projects. As a result, you may accelerate your growth while decreasing your effort without sacrificing quality.

The files listed below will be pre-installed when your application is produced, and the formats for each application file will remain constant.

2. Install Django App

After you've established your program, the following step is to install it.

As a result, you must edit the settings.py file.

Keep in mind that you will be modifying the primary settings.py file of your Django project, not the one in the app directory.

After you have added the program to the list of Installed Apps, you will just need to put its name in the INSTALLED APPS list.

Congratulations, you have successfully deployed a custom Django application.

You must now include the app in your urls.py file so that anybody who searches the app's URL in a browser will access the app above.

2. Install Django App

You will need to create some code to incorporate the app in urls.py.

To begin, create a new Python file in the demo directory and paste the following code into it.

```
1    from django.urls import path
2
3    from . import views
4
5    urlpatterns = [
6        path('', views.index, name='index'),
7    ]
```

With the above code, you are informing the Django project that you must call this method in the views.py file.

Don't worry; you'll be altering that file as well.

You imported the django.urls package and path function from there in the preceding code.

The path () method is a new feature in Django 2.0. It is preferable to update if you have any older versions.

This function takes two inputs. The first is the URL that was found and transmitted to the URL bar by the browser. The other parameter is to execute the file or program, which is an index function.

You will now modify the urls.py file in the main Django project.

There is just one item in the list, and you must add the new data.

```python
from django.contrib import admin
from django.urls import include, path

urlpatterns = [
    path('admin/', admin.site.urls),
]
```

After the inclusion of the app urls.

```python
urlpatterns = [
    path('demo/', include('demo.urls')),
    path('admin/', admin.site.urls),
]
```

By completing the next step, you'll be making the system direct your server to search the URL for the demo term. Finally, inside the sample application directory, point the URL to the urls.py file.

4. Building the views.py file

Next, you'll construct the Django project's views file. This file will generate a browser view.

Just utilize this code snippet, which is already included in the demo directory and views.py file.

```python
from django.http import HttpResponse
def index(request):
    return HttpResponse("DataFlair Django Tutorial<html><body><h1> Hello World DataFlair Dango tutorials</body></html>")
```

According to its name, this is the file where you will generate views that the browser will display.

As you can see, you will import a HttpResponse function and also build a function named index, which will be used in the urls.py file.

The function receives the request in the same method a server would interact with the server. You'll be returning HttpResponse(), and everything you specify in the function's parameter will be deployed by the browser.

There are no more answers other than the HttpResponse, which you will use in the future.

If you've done everything correctly up to this point, you've just finished building your first Django App and website.

You may now access the admin app if you like, but it will be discussed in the following phase.

If your app does not launch, enter the following command into the URL:

localhost:8000/demo/

This part taught you more about Django's file structure and how to build your first project. Don't worry if the program fails to start; there might be some issues. Just go through this section again.

Django Admin Interface

The Django Admin interface is the most visible element of the Django Framework, and the ease it provides to site administrators is significant. Moreover, it is an essential component of the Django Framework and will assist you in a variety of ways.

Let's start with the website's Admin Interface.

As the name implies, the Admin interface is the engine of your project. Site administrators use this to add, remove, and alter material on the site. Moreover, it is utilized to manage additional developer-created functionality.

There is one tough component; the admin interface is the major controller, and it must be developed by the developer separately. It would help if you managed everything, from database connection to improving the security of the admin interface, since anybody who uses it is a controller, and any vulnerability left will be disastrous for your website.

Interacting with Django Admin Interface

Django Admin is a kind of interface that is intended to suit all of the demands of developers. Its language is quite generic.

The Django Admin includes a comprehensive interface, so you won't have to bother about creating one for your project. To begin, learn the process of putting up a Django Admin site since you will need it in future projects.

Getting Ready Django Admin Site

You should take these steps to establish the Django Admin Site and run user models.

1. Launch the Django server, then type localhost:8000/admin/ into the URL bar.

The site should display an image and prompt you for your login and password. You may now continue to create one.

2. Launch PowerShell or the terminal and terminate the server by pressing CTRL + C.

Then, enter the following command:

```
python manage.py createsuperuser
```

3. After running the above program, you will be prompted to input a username, which should be your chosen option. Next, it will ask you for your email address and password. As a result, you

should be able to finish the details without difficulty.

There are various built-in security mechanisms, such as generating a complicated password if your password is numeric, and many other security issues have been addressed for users.

Superuser

A superuser is an admin for your website who can do any data modification and content alteration related to your website.

Moreover, since the superuser information is your website's essential driver, you should never divulge or share them with anybody. While the website is operational, it is vital for administering and controlling your website.

After successfully creating the superuser, you will return to the admin page to restart your Django server.

1. Log in to admin using the credentials you established.

You will see the choices and a lovely interface:

Since the custom apps aren't registered with the Django admin interface, none of them will be shown. There are just two fields here, and each one has two alternatives.

3. Now, choose the users field, and you should see something similar to this.

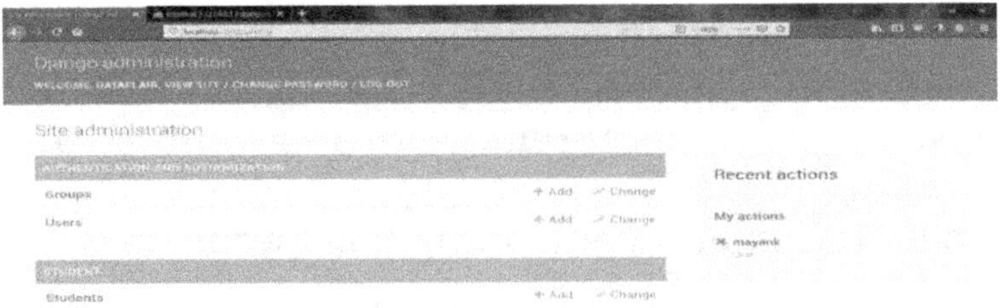

You should only see one user and the information you entered despite the fact that you wouldn't be able to see the password.

All passwords are encrypted using a unique key in the settings.py file, which is a benefit for Django.

3. Verify that the user you created was saved.

4. Now launch phpmyadmin and go to the Django project database you created. Next, if you access the auth users table, you will see all of the data except the password.

You will also see that there are other tables in the database that you did not create. Don't worry; these are all the imported model tables from the Django.contrib package. The Django.contrib refers to a Django package that is comparable to the relation of the standard library in Python. The Django.contrib package contains almost all of the necessary functionality.

5. Return to the Django Project's main page.

6. Next, open the file admin.py of your program. The structure of \sthe directory should look like way:

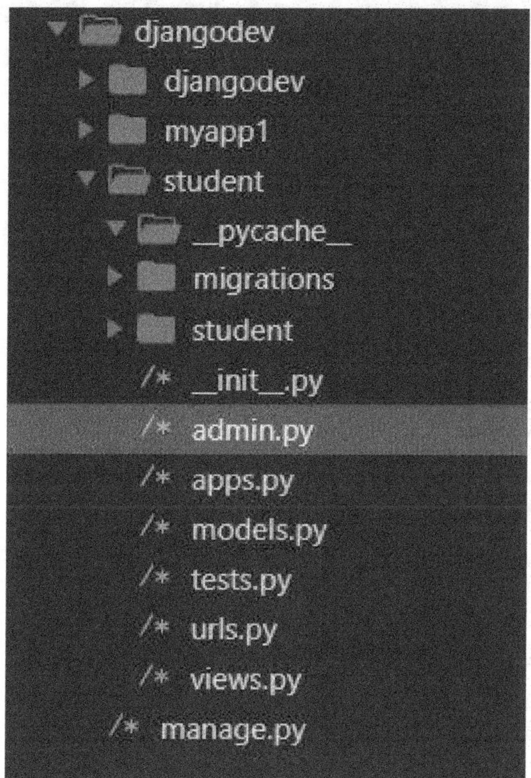

7. Open the admin.py file and add the following two lines:

```python
from .models import Student

admin.site.register(Student)
```

The first sentence is used to import the Student class or the custom model that was generated.

The second line sends the model to the Django Admin interface or registers it.

8. Now, when you open admin again, it will not prompt you for a password.

You've got the student model in admin, so go ahead and open that student field.

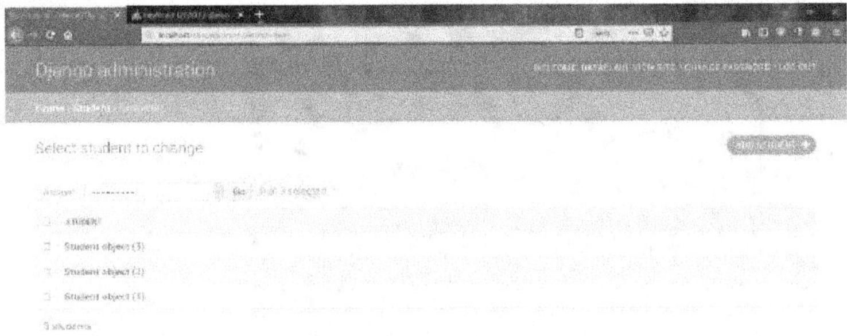

You'll see a list of your pupils, and you'll be able to access important options such as add a new student.

Adding a new student will produce a new record in your database; all of it is the duty of the

Django Admin interface that integrates with Django ORM.

9. Then, choose any student object.

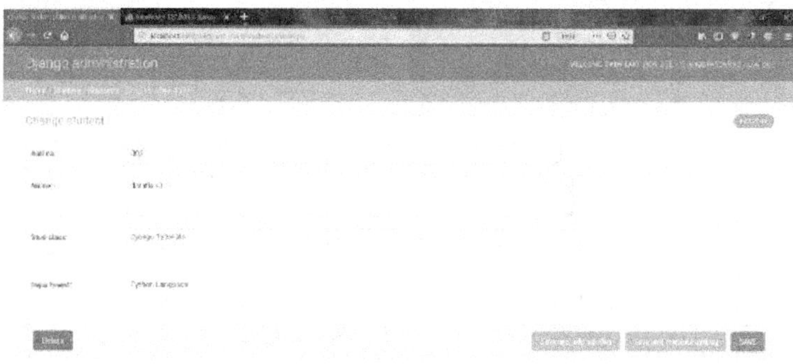

Without entering the database, you may instantly view and alter the information.

Additionally, you should notice numerous choices, such as save and delete.

See the power it gives you without having to create the Django Admin interface. In other words, it's simpler to use and more secure than everything else you've tried.

If you have multiple developers working on the same assignment, then more interface functionality will be essential. You may pick which developers receive certain rights without having to do anything.

In conclusion, the Django Admin Interface is an excellent tool; nevertheless, many websites may not need an admin interface due to its nature. Nevertheless, that will not be very scalable or commercially viable. Suppose you want speedy content management without having to reinvent the wheel. In that case, Django is the most excellent framework to use and the best admin you can get, with many capabilities as a developer.

This chapter has walked you through the process of creating a superuser and how to link your project with the Admin interface. It would help if you experimented with several models using admin to get comfortable with it.

Django Database

This section will look at connecting databases to the Django project.

While developing a web project or any sort of project, you will need some form of feedback from end-users or customers. Databases now handle all of the data submitted by customers. In the present day, it is hard to create a website without first creating a database. Even if it's only a blog, you'll need a database.

To achieve this, you will need software. The purpose of this program is to store such data effectively and also some middleware that can enable you to interface with the database.

Connecting Your Database with Django Project

When you built the first app and launched the server, you undoubtedly noticed a new file in your project directory. 'db.sqlite3' is the name of this file. The file is a database file that will store all of the data that you produce.

```
myblog
write
db.sqlite3
manage
```

This file is produced automatically since Django's default database configuration is SQLite. Although it is helpful for testing and has many advantages, if you want a scalable website, you should switch to an efficient database.

In this scenario, you will be utilizing MySQL, and this part will show you how to integrate your project with MYSQL.

Databases Dictionary Indexes

To begin, open the settings.py file in your web application/project and look for the following section:

```python
# Database
# https://docs.djangoproject.com/en/2.1/ref/settings/#databases

DATABASES = {
    'default': {
        'ENGINE': 'django.db.backends.sqlite3',
        'NAME': os.path.join(BASE_DIR, 'db.sqlite3'),
    }
}
```

A database is a pre-defined dictionary in Django Framework with the index value 'default' for the major database where all data is maintained.

You can have several databases since you require data backups, but the default database is just one, and you won't be adding many databases right now.

The default includes a dictionary with two indexes:

Engine

It defines the library that will be utilized once linked to a certain website. "Django.db.backends.sqlite3" should be the value. This is a Python library for the sqlite3 database that will adapt your Python code to the database language.

As a result, you don't need to learn a new database language, and you can locate all of the code in Python.

Name

This section contains the name and path of the database that you are utilizing. This option varies depending on the kind of database you're using. You may try the database file here.

You will also provide the name of the database file or db.sqlite3 if it is not accessible. If you modify the name to db1.sqlite3 or anything else, the server will produce that file in your root directory every time you run it.

As you can see, creating a database using the Django framework is not difficult. Note that each database includes characteristics that become the default dictionary indexes that you may generate dependent on the database you are connected to.

Django and MySQL

MYSQL is a powerful database that offers several capabilities and flexibility. Here's how to include it in your project.

1. First, install Xampp.

Xampp is a free, open-source utility that comes with the Apache server and PhpMyAdmin, which is the appropriate source for beginner programmers to work with MySQL.

Click the following link to download XAMPP.

https://www.apachefriends.org/download.html

2. Launch the Xampp control panel.

Following installation, enter the Xampp Control Panel and start Apache and MySQL.

Run the Apache server first, then the MySQL server.

Just click the start button to bring up the following image:

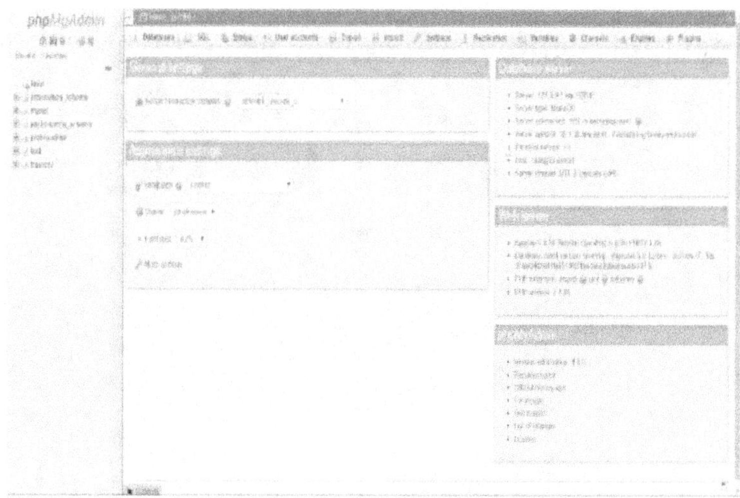

Next, click the Admin of the MySQL Service, which should bring up a web page.

This is the primary page where you will monitor your database.

The benefit of Xampp is that it has a robust interactive environment, and the time of deploying your model, that too will take place here.

As a result, you will have an effective database for your project. That's a piece of cake.

Just click the new button, as seen below. Finally, enter the name of your database and press the create button.

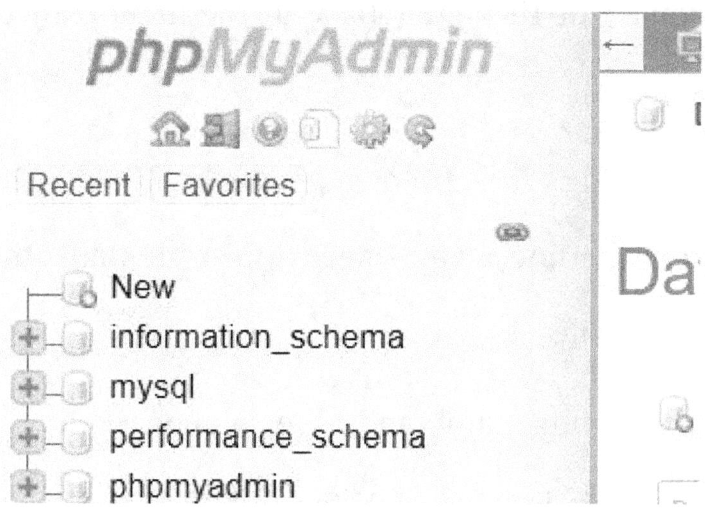

After you're finished, it will add your database to the list.

That's all; you don't need to do anything more. You will simply be working with Python, and Django's model component will prepare everything.

3. Modifying settings.py

In the next final step, you will be altering the dictionary of the \sdatabase in the main project settings.py.

By entering the following command at the command line, you need first install the following file:

By using this command, the Django code for connecting to the MySql database will be installed.

Next, in settings.py, swap this code with the DATABASE dictionary.

```
DATABASES = {
    'default': {
        'ENGINE': 'django.db.backends.mysql',
        'NAME': 'dataflair',
        'USER': 'root',
        'PASSWORD': '',
        'HOST': '',
        'PORT': '',
        'OPTIONS': {
            'init_command': "SET sql_mode='STRICT_TRANS_TABLES'"
        }
    }
}
```

In this situation, the properties are more numerous since Mysql adds functionalities to sqlite3. The engine in this example is "Django.db.backends.mysql," which is the same name as the Python package for MYSQL.

To prevent errors, it's best to leave the password field blank.

In the above example, the HOST is the host server; however, when left blank, the localhost is used as the default.

OPTIONS is a fascinating feature. You're just providing the SQL as a string via Python, which the SQL server will read afterward.

Fill in the blanks with the following:

```
SET sql_mode = 'STRICT_TRANS_TABLES'
```

Essentially, SQL is given as a string.

Execute the following instructions to complete the process:

```
python manage.py migrate
python manage.py runserver
```

After that, reload the phpMyAdmin page to see certain tables appear.

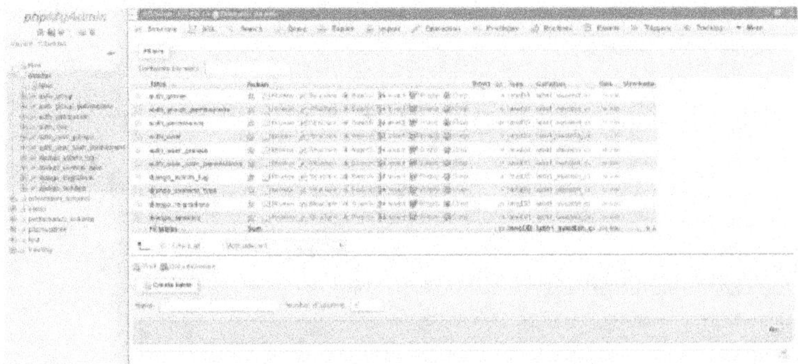

You're done! You now have everything set for your website. The assembly of the components and pieces is now complete.

Chapter 15: Tips for Django and Python Beginners

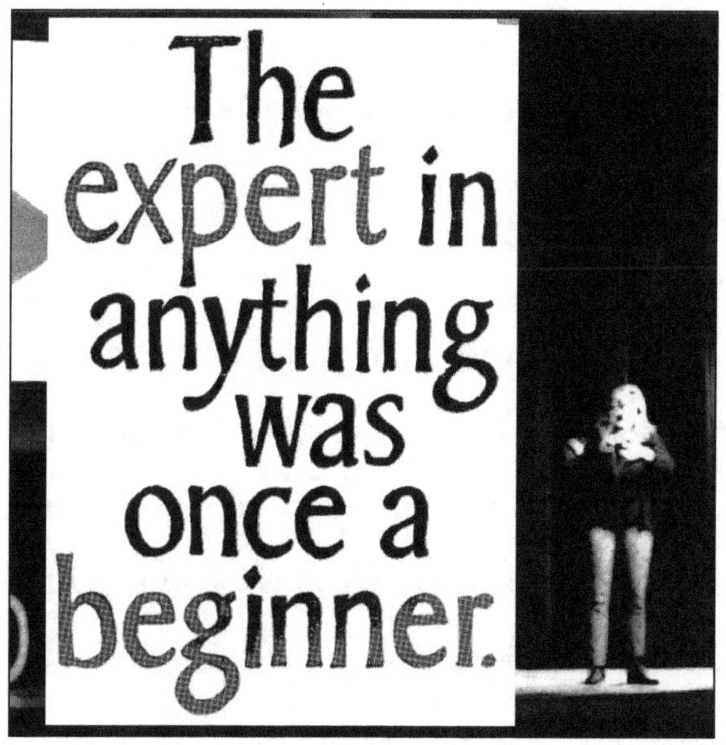

So, you've decided to learn Python or Django. Or perhaps you're already familiar with the language and framework. These are strategies that can help you speed up your learning.

1. Master the Rubrics

It would help if you mastered your primary. And, thanks to Python syntax, you can use Django without being a Python expert because it is friendly to new programmers. Python code is similar to English.

Despite its simple syntax, the fundamentals cannot be overlooked. The path to fully understanding Django begins with mastering the fundamentals. So, as your first step toward becoming a Django expert, make sure you learn the fundamentals.

2. Begin to Solve Problems

You've mastered the fundamentals. You now have a solid understanding of the Python programming language. It is time to start working out little concerns.

Come up with a function that can calculate taxes. Create a loop that prompts the user to input his or her age until the user exits the circle, at which point the average of all ages is computed.

There are some websites where you can do small tasks. Afterward, based on the response, you receive points and begin to graduate.

CodeWars is one such website.

3. Create small, simple projects

If you can solve modest issues, why not start constructing fun projects?

If you have learned how to utilize Python to address more significant problems, now is the time to offer yourself a more challenging task.

The plan is to start with simple Python programs and gradually raise the degree of complexity. But do not attempt to establish a YouTube-style project on your own.

Just begin by creating something straightforward that you will love working on. A game of tic-tac-toe or a number guessing game.

After you're finished, make another one. Or start putting new features to the one you've developed.

I realize it will take time, and you will have to spend a lot of time Googling, but that is how the finest coders begin.

Start with a Flask

If you have never learned a programming language or web development and want to learn Django, a nice place to start is with a flask.

Flask is a wonderful alternative to Django. It's more precise and easier to grasp.

Flask is fantastic for the beginning since it offers more features, but you must apply them.

With a flask, what you see is what you get. Nothing else. And it's really simple.

Dive into Web Development with Django

After you have mastered the fundamentals of the Python programming language and have created your first tiny projects, now, you're ready to study Django.

Master New Django Concepts

You've learned how to start a Django project. You are aware of how the Model View Template operates. Yet there's still a lot to learn. So much more.

The key is to understand new ideas like Signals, Logging, Testing, and so on.

Keep in mind that this is not a race. Take time to read the documentation.

Try it. Don't even try to memorize. But first, discover how it works. What components are moving, why should you utilize that notion, and when should you use it?

And then...

Start Applying Those New Concepts

Use what you've learned as soon as possible. There is no better way to assimilate anything than to put it into practice straight soon.

Create a little pet project where you may employ it, or better yet, incorporate it into your present one.

Read Code from Experts

If you want to become an excellent Django developer, you must study code written by pros.

The internet is a fantastic source of knowledge. Why don't you get Django Github projects to study?

You may still download and enhance the project. And in order to do so, you must read, read, read, and learn the code.

Surround Yourself with People Learning

When you surround yourself with individuals who are studying the same language as you, it gives you a feeling of camaraderie. In other words, you're all working for the same objective, and you can rely on one another. It's possible that one of your pals fixed your issue a few days ago. Why not ask him how he came up with the answer?

Surround Yourself with Experts

To become the greatest, you need both your peers and specialists. Your friends, coworkers, and mentors who have used Django or Python can solve difficult issues that novice coders cannot.

A specialist can fix your difficulties and see the larger picture.

A novice can show you how to accomplish something, but only an expert can judge whether your current approach is ideal.

Read Lots of Django Books

It may be difficult to surround oneself with professionals at times, or you may not have time to communicate with them due to the nature of the work they perform.

Fortunately, it is not the end. These experts have authored several books.

What's fascinating about books is that you can learn something in hours that pros take years to learn.

Although these books will not make you a Django expert, they will put you on the right track to becoming a decent developer.

Write Code Every Day

It would help if you coded every day. You decide how much.

Single moms may have a more difficult time setting apart time than teens. Individuals who spend most of the day outdoors working have little time to code. People who work as programmers must also devote time outside of work to coding.

Every day, even if it's just for 20 minutes, make time to code.

Making coding a daily habit can help you become a better programmer.

Take Some Breaks

After a long time of studying, you need to take pauses.

Taking pauses enables your brain to relax and arrange what you've learned.

It's easy to lose your perspective on the greater goal and lock yourself into a piece of code. After you've been studying for 2 hours nonstop, it's simple to get dissatisfied because a certain subject isn't seeping into your brain.

As a result, you should take a break and return refreshed.

Ask Other People

You won't know much while you're learning. Or maybe you don't understand how they function. You will have a lot of coding-related inquiries. And the greatest way to solve things is to ask.

Just asking folks can teach you a lot. Post your query in coding forums. Consult your coworkers. And don't be scared to ask. Remember, it's better to ask a stupid question than not ask at all and put yourself in danger.

You can learn if you ask.

Teach Your Friends

Teaching is a great method to learn something new.

As you learn something, you comprehend how to apply it. Yet, while training others, you must understand how to utilize it and how it functions within. What it does on the backend, what happens if you do this, what happens if you skip this, and why the developers designed it to operate this way and no other way.

As you educate others, there is so much to learn and discover.

These are the steps you should take to become a skilled Python coder. It is now your responsibility to follow them.

Conclusion

Now that you're done reading this book, we hope that it's been amazing and you've learned lots of Python principles and its Django framework. If you like to study in a more participatory manner, you might look into some online lessons.

Note that although Django is a popular framework, there are alternative frameworks for web development, and depending on the kind of project, you may choose to use a different framework.

But, if you believe you've achieved a strong foundation in Python and Django foundations, you might embrace a new challenge by expanding your knowledge by reading intermediate to advanced books.